Appointment with Ying @ 8am
STARTING UP A BUSINESS
by YING SA

To Riley!

Make it big!

Oct 2021

Published by:
TRAITMARKER BOOKS
2984 Del Rio Pike
Franklin, TN 37069
traitmarkerbooks.com
traitmarker@gmail.com

ATTRIBUTIONS
Interior Text Font: Minion Pro
Interior Title Fonts: Minion Pro
Editor: Sharilyn S. Grayson
Advisor: Steven Hou
Cover Design: Grace Yang
Cover Photo: Stevin Dahl

PUBLISHING DATA:
ISBN: 978-1-64713-329-0

Printed in the United States of America

Appointment with Ying @ 8am
STARTING UP A BUSINESS

by YING SA

To my husband, Steve
who is always my most
important appointment

Contents

PREFACE

A FISH STORY

In September 2002, a couple who owned a local Asian fish market came to my house on a Saturday. At the time, I was running a home office CPA practice outside of my full-time job. I did not know them in person other than seeing them in the market every time I shopped there. Peter and Meg Keobunta were Laotian immigrants who operated one of the largest fish markets in town.

They told me that one of their friends had told them that I was the only person who could help them. I welcomed them to my home office, where I helped many other Asian clients needing CPA services. The Keobuntas were about to say something but broke down to cry, both of them.

My two girls at age 4 and 2 were excited about our guests, but now seeing them sad, the girls suddenly stopped jumping and stood quietly gazing at the Keobuntas.

This couple's helpless fears were coming through their trembling hands, and they were in a state of irreconcilable sorrow for a long time. I had no words. My girls brought them water.

Finally, the Keobuntas said: "The fish."

I learned that they had an attorney who had told them to admit everything so the fish case could be done quickly. Following the attorney's advice, the couple, who had very limited English proficiency, signed all the papers without getting any explanation. The Keobunta case was concluded in August that year, but the couple ended up being charged so severely that they were in the stage of shock.

They were here with me.

They had been charged with commercializing wildlife. This is the same charge to bring against someone who sells a wild deer horn or elephant tusk. In this case, it would be the charge for someone who took wild fish from the river to sell them for profit. But that is not what happened.

The location of the Keobunta's market is near a homeless shelter. Some homeless people would wander over and ask for something or some money. The couple were soft-hearted and never turned anyone away empty-handed.

During this summer, a couple of homeless folks brought some fish over to the store to exchange for money. As a mercy to homeless people, Peter and Meg bought the fish from them for a dollar and sold them for $1.20 a tail.

This was not some grand scheme to use up all the wild fish in the river. And the fish the homeless people caught were the same species of fish that Peter and Meg bought all the time from distributors in Chicago. Peter and Meg were not stealing from public lands or endangering their customers. They had only been trying to be kind.

"It was the same fish," Meg cried.

"We were just trying to help the homeless. We do not even know fish can be different," Peter added.

JUSTICE FOR ALL

I had to help Peter and Meg. This was a misunderstanding that had turned into an injustice.

Later I learned that their legal representation was so inadequate that the couple was advised to plead guilty to all counts without a translator and without knowing what the charges were. As the result of that, each received a one-year suspended sentence. They were fined $500 on each count ($20,000 total fines for both) and ordered to pay a restitution, a civil penalty of $15.00 for each of the 348 fish bought or seized by the government agents (most of which were, as later proven, actually the Market's regular inventory from the Chicago distributors), plus surcharges and court costs. Summed up, the cost looked to be around $39,000.

As a start, I called Peter and Meg's attorney. I explained my understanding of the case and then I asked, "How can they be charged so severely? I could not make any sense of this case; could you..."

The attorney hung up the phone.

With that click, my work began. For the next four years, I used all of my free time to help Peter and Meg. I worked to overturn this case with help from a free legal clinic and help from local community leaders and government officials. I used my PTO, my sick days, my weekends, and my vacation time from my full-time job to visit community leaders and state government officials, sitting in every meeting there was with the free legal clinic professors and students.

Through the hard work of the clinic, myself, and others, the facts that were ignored by the prior attorney came to light. I dug through years of invoices for the store that Peter and Meg ran. Finally, I was able to find the invoices from distributors in Chicago, which proved that the couple had been purchasing the same fish to sell for years. I could match the invoices against the sales records to show that most of the fish sold at the store had been bought from distributors. Only a few were wild.

Once we showed the court the invoices for the fish that had been bought legally, the case could not stand. In October 2007, the case was overturned, the sentence dropped, and the money refunded.

HEAVEN SENT

Peter was so relieved that his legal ordeal was over after four years. I was, too. I had invested so much of my emotion in this case. I cried at the time Peter and Meg cried their happy tears.

Peter called and said: "I want to buy you a car; I got my money back today in the mail."

I was so thrilled that he got his refund back so quickly, but I told him, "I do not need a car, and don't worry about paying me."

I did not need a reward. I was touched to witness that the USA is not just a land of opportunity. It is also a place where justice and fairness are at the heart of this amazing government.

But Peter did not give in. The next thing I knew, he renovated his next-door warehouse base into an office for me. He said to me: "You need to come out of your house. We need you here so we can have your protection and help to run our business." Just before I could ask him for how much rent he would charge me, as if he read my mind, he said: "No rent for a year."

Community CPA was born. Not like most of the professional firms labeled by the experts' last name. The brand name of this business is no one but "the Community."

From that moment, appointments became the way of life for me. When you are being regarded as "heaven sent" by the community, how could you not be fully committed to being your best?

Community CPA was meant to happen, and I and my staff just happened to exist at the right time with the right circumstance. We chose to ride the ups and downs while poised to enjoy the expansion of the firm.

Peter Keobunta became one of my biggest advocates. He referred his friends by sending them to me. My way of life was shaped by the needs of immigrant communities. When people asked Peter how he knew of me, he pointed up at the sky and said: "Heaven, up there." When people ask him when they can see me, he said: "You have to make appointment with her."

Are you ready for your appointment?

If you ask my husband about what I do every day so far in my life, he will say, "She is in appointments all day long and all the time." That is so true. I love to meet with people, and having these appointments is such a vital part of my being!

In fact, for the past ten years, I have held over 15,600 appointments with my clients. Though those appointments represent a large investment of my time, I have learned as much from my clients as they learned from me. In this book, *Appointment with Ying @ 8am,* I want to share with you some important business principles regarding starting a business that I discovered through my experiences with my clients.

I hope you will enjoy this book. I am working on three other books right now, and I hope at the end of this book you are energized to go to the second one. I labeled my books with times in a day. This book is at 8am; then the second one is at 10am; then 2pm, and finally 6pm.

As the sun rises and sets, this is the natural rhythm of a day. Business, like any other thing in life, has a rhythm, too. I plan to talk about developing the business you started @ 10am; business expansion or sun setting @ 2pm, and finally @ 6pm the new way of retirement.

The book is the beginning of a *series* of four different times. The title itself tells you that you and I are face to face. You are asking for my time to teach you. So you are at the center of this book. I thank you and all of my clients for the birth of this book and the three upcoming ones.

But before we can get to those future books, we need to learn the lessons from this one. It's time now for an appointment with me to learn about starting a business at 8am.

MEETING WITH IMMIGRANTS

I have had many appointments with immigrant business owners. After all, I'm an immigrant myself. Their questions come from being unfamiliar with the way things are done in the USA, which is different from the way things are done in their home countries.

Living in a different country before you come to the USA gives you certain expectations. You get used to the way things work where everything is familiar to you. Then, when you go to a different place, you have to adjust to a different way of life. Rules, regulations, and laws not only are different, but in some cases are totally unexpected to these newcomers.

What I do in many appointments is the job of explaining differences. English is my second language, too; so I do not have big words to utter to my immigrant business clients.

Our immigrant business clients are from 29 different countries, and the magic we have in our firm is that we speak 9 different languages collectively. Even if we do not speak a particular language, as a firm, we have the reputation of speaking a special kind of English that all of our clients would understand. One of our clients told his friend so, when his friend was worried about meeting us, as his English is not very good.

Language is not a barrier to me. Instead, it is a bridge for me to connect with my clients. I love seeing the smile on my clients' faces when they understand the nature of the issue and find the solution to the problem right in the hour of our appointment.

THE BUSINESS IMMIGRANT

There is another kind of immigrant that I also meet.

After having thousands of appointments, I have seen a new kind of immigrant on the rise: these are folks who were born and raised in USA but were never exposed to business concepts at home around the dinner table. They needed me as much as those who are new to the country. For those folks, they have grown up their whole lives in the USA, with great-great-great-great-grand-fathers born in this country, but they are truly immigrants to the Land of Business. Everything is just as new to a new American business owner as it is to an immigrant to this country.

If you are new to business, you are a business immigrant.

You may have a hard time thinking of yourself as an immigrant. You may think that because you are born in USA and you speak perfect English, you will naturally start any businesses with no problem.

You have it all wrong.

In the world of doing business, speaking English well and being born in the USA offers you some convenience but does not give you a free visa to guarantee success.

Here are three truths about language in business.

First, everyone can access the translation app that puts all people on a level playing field. In business, language is the smallest denominator. It does not impact the life of the business as much as 30 years ago.

Second, the USA has a multicultural heritage that has always been multilingual. We are a melting pot. Look at the foreign language newspapers that have always been printed on American soil just for immigrants – German, Russian, Chinese, Spanish, and Italian in past centuries, and dozens of languages now. Speaking other languages without English is already part of the American experience.

Third, businesses of all sizes are going global now. Think of a small startup online retail business that orders products from ten different countries and retails them online to Americans. Imagine how multilingual the employees would have to be. The size of your business does not relate to how global you will have to be.

In starting a business, native English speakers and new Americans are in the same situation. All are immigrants to the Land of

Business. And all equally need guidance through the process of starting a business.

I love working with immigrants and business immigrants! I am good at making complex rules and laws very simple so that anyone can understand them. I have a very soft heart towards immigrants of all kinds. If you are new to business, you have come to the right place!

I am glad you are here for this 8am appointment with me.

HOW I CAN HELP YOU

Here is what is important. No one has a perfect set of expectations. Everyone has something to learn about beginning a business. No matter what language you speak or what kind of business background you have, you do not have the whole truth about how to succeed at your business.

But I am here to help! I can offer you a few very valuable things during our time together, during your own *Appointment with Ying @ 8am.*

I can help you:

Take an honest look at your business cultural background. I can help you understand your expectations. I can help you see how your background will influence your choices as you start your business.

Explore the kind of business you want to start. I will help you anticipate what you can expect. Working through the *Reflections* in this book will help you prepare for your specific kind of startup.

Make a roadmap of what to do to get started. I have clients who have come to appointments and taken a hand-lettered roadmap of the steps of starting a business. Fifteen years later, my handwriting has already grown older; they still have these roadmaps with steps checked off them.

If you have fears or questions about immigrating to the Land of Business, then I can help you answer your questions and quiet your fears so that you are ready to become a citizen of the Land of Business.

I meet many people each day, and I am emotionally invested in my clients. My heart and soul embrace them. I work hard to bring blessings to my clients. I am an ordinary human, but I live to help my clients. I am not as smart as Elon Musk, but I work no less than he does.

Throughout the years, I have found myself repeating some important business principles and knowledge to clients.

As a firm, we have done many seminars in the Midwest. We organized a nonprofit organization called Immigrant Entrepreneur Summit to spread the knowledge of business to the immigrant population. Still, I have a desire to reach more. My passion to help everyone navigate life in business has led me to write this book.

I hope you find yourself in the book and that you find the solution to your life situation. I hope my clients see what else I do other than what I did for them. I hope they realize that I have done so much more in business so they can deepen their love for our firm.

I also want my children to know more about what their mom did during the time she was so busy with work. In this book, I want to give them another dimension of mom's life so they can realize how fulfilled I was and am and will be in my life's journey.

Circumstances in my adulthood have led me to a way of life that I would never have imagined in my youth. I am so grateful at every event in my own life, and I hope that once you finish reading this book, you too will know the answer and know the purpose and know the beauty of discovering the unmanifested possibilities that could unfold at any time and any day in your life. You are reading this book for a reason. Just prepare yourself.

WHAT YOU WILL LEARN IN THIS BOOK

In this book, I will tell you stories about my appointments. I love my clients, and in order to keep their identities private, I have changed their names and the details of their businesses. If you are one of my clients, you will not find any of your secrets in this book. But you will find situations common to most of you, and you will find my respect for you and my hopes for your continued success. You are part of my happy life.

Each of these stories shows a truth or principle about business in a way that is easy to understand. You will see how no two business owners are exactly alike and how each business owner starts business with a different set of expectations. Some of them work, and some of them do not. All of my clients have to adjust their expectations in some way. And watching them do that is a lot more entertaining and understandable than listening to someone give you facts and rules.

In this book, you will meet people who are very dear to me. My client Jose is from Mexico. He has made his choices in business by doing the next necessary, possible thing. My clients Emily and Hua Hua are very smart ladies. They have been able to start different kinds of business and respond to setbacks in creative ways. You will also meet Stacie, and you have already met Peter and Meg. Their concern, even though they want success in business, is to benefit the people around them.

I will also tell you stories about entrepreneurs I admire. Donald Trump has important truths to share about business strategy, while Elon Musk shows us the way to make useful products that support a unique vision. Eckhart Tolle teaches us about the personal aspect of business. Their stories about business may also tell you something about yourself. I will share quotes from other successful business leaders, too.

So keep your eyes open to see which of my clients and which of these famous business entrepreneurs you are most like. See the mistakes they make and the challenges they face. And find encouragement in the fact that despite facing setbacks and dealing with problems, they are all successful in business. You can be, too.

Let's begin your *Appointment with Ying @ 8am!*

CHAPTER 1

Do I Need a Business Background to Start a Business?

WE ARE ALL BUSINESS IMMIGRANTS

Do you need a business background to start a business? The truth is that few people who start a business for the first time have a business background. When you start a business for the first time, unless business has been part of your daily life from childhood, you are so new to this experience that you might as well think that you are an immigrant to the Land of Business. You have the same need for practical knowledge and experience as anyone else.

"But Ying," you might say in your perfect English, "I have a college degree in business. I am ready to put it to work!"

If you have done the work to get a business degree, I am proud of you! Your degree took a lot of studying, a lot of time, and a lot of money. Good for you!

But you are still a business immigrant. You are in the same situation as an immigrant to the USA. That immigrant knows a lot about the USA, but there are things that he or she does not know and will not know except through experiences. Only experiences of daily business life in the USA teach a person about real business life in the USA.

You are like a person who has studied China for many years but never visited. You may know the history and the language, but you have never breathed the air or shaken hands with the people. You are not Chinese until you live in China and belong there.

It is important for you to recognize this truth so that you can avoid trouble from thinking that your degree and your English would mean that you know how to start a business.

For everybody else, be cheerful! You do not need a business background to run a business. The rules and the culture of the Land of Business may take time for you to learn, but you can learn them. How do I know this? I know from experience in the real world: the experiences of my own life, my client's lives, and the lives of people I admire.

All of these immigrants to the Land of Business come from one of three imaginary countries: the Country of the Hand, the Country of the Heart, or the Country of the Head. Knowing which kind of country you come from and which kind of passport you hold is very important during your journey to the Land of Business. If you do not know, that ignorance will cost you.

From my years of experience, I can tell by the questions my clients ask and the concerns they have which imaginary countries they are from and what kind of passport they hold. For me, despite of all the different languages they speak, they all come from one of the three places: the Country of the Hand, the Country of the Heart, or the Country of the Head.

THE COUNTRY OF THE HAND

The business immigrant from the Country of the Hand is represented by a land animal. Hand people are "handlike" because 1) they are stable, 2) they are productive, and 3) they can be relied upon. For this reason, I think of hand people like horses because they do practical work, they are strong and hard-working, and they keep their eyes on the work before them.

Clients who come from the Country of the Hand want to start a business because they are very good at what they do. They feel a drive inside to do the particular work that they do. They could be a talented landscaper with a passion for seeing plants grow in beautiful ways, or a gifted seamstress who can make marvelous dresses and suits, or an artisan baker who makes delicate croissants and hearty loaves.

For someone from the Country of the Hand, the end result of the work – the product - is the most important thing to them. They figure that if they pay enough attention to the product, the business details will take care of themselves.

THE COUNTRY OF THE HEART

The business immigrant from the Country of the Heart is represented by a water animal. Heart people are like "water" in several ways: 1) they are deep, 2) they are mysterious, and 3) they "go with the flow." For this reason, I think of heart people like dolphins because dolphins are friendly creatires, live in groups, and look out for each other.

When my clients from the Country of the Heart begin talking, they focus on other people. Sometimes, they are very concerned to benefit customers in some way, to revitalize a damaged neighborhood, or to give away much of their profits to charity.

These are people who talk about sharing profits with employees. Some of them insist on paying employees when there is no money to pay the business owner themselves. For these clients from the Country of the Heart, the kind of business is not as important as the benefit it can bring to others.

THE COUNTRY OF THE HEAD

The business immigrant from the Country of the Head is represented by an air animal. Head people are like "air" in the following ways: 1) they have a "birds eye" view of things, 2) they have a grasp on details that others can't see, and 3) they are calculated. For this reason, I think of head people as owls because owls are solitary creatures, they are often heard but not seen, and they are considered wise.

The business immigrants from the Country of the Head are different from the other two. For them, the important thing is not the kind of business or the benefit that a business can bring to others. For them, the important thing is the bottom line – making a lot of money. They are starting a business to build as much profit as possible.

Some of them think of business as a kind of game, and they look at a strong profit as a sign that they are winning that game. So they could start a bakery or a computer store and be equally happy, as long as they are making money.

I can hear you thinking about the clients from these different countries. "Ying, how could anyone just be concerned with money?" some might say. Others might say, "Ying, I don't understand how you could start a business unless you loved what you did every day. Why else would you start a business?" Or some might say, "Ying, those people who want to give everything away are just crazy! Who does that?"

Good! If you are having those thoughts, then you are learning which country you are from. Which assumptions do you have about business? How do you expect it to work? What is most important for you when you start a business? If you are thinking that two of the other kinds of immigrants are a little foolish, then you can begin to understand what kind of business immigrant you are.

THE BURN LEVEL IN YOUR HEART

Take me, for instance. As far as business is concerned, I come from the Country of the Heart. What is most important to me is the welfare of the people around me.

I came from a very simple background. Born in the Red China

of the 1960s, I was educated and raised under communist principles. I was not born in a business entrepreneur family. My social circle had always looked down at commerce people.

The China I grew up within was a place where the communist spirit shone through all things. I never dreamed to be a businessperson, and I would have been ashamed if I ever did. Everything was modeled after Mao's communist sharing spirit.

Before the Burn

In China in the 1970s, my family did not use money for everyday living; we lived on tickets that were like ration cards. We received tickets for fabric, tickets for meat, and tickets for Napa cabbages. If you wanted to buy something with money, you had to have a ticket for permission to buy it. No ticket, no product - no matter how much money you had. That was how everything stayed fair.

Our family had even more tickets than others. Because we are Mongolians – a minority in China -- we got more meat tickets than the regular Han Chinese families.

You didn't buy these tickets. You were given them. Advertising didn't even exist because no one really bought anything – not in the way capitalists bought things.

Life was all the same until one day, I saw a magazine.

Dad was a professor at The Foreign Affairs College in Beijing, where he taught French and English literature when I was in my teens. His students became diplomats who served at embassies all over the world. I still remember how his job introduced me to things about the western world that I could not understand.

One day after school, I found a large, glossy magazine on his desk. Dad had taken it home to read. The colors and unusual print quality attracted me; the smooth, silky feeling of the paper was very unusual. I flipped the pages. They were in French.

All of a sudden, in front of me I saw this beautiful, naked lady sitting sideways in a see-through bathtub. I asked Dad, "What is she doing?"

Dad raised his head and looked at what I was seeing. He said, "Oh, that is an advertisement. The soap company is selling soap."

"What do you mean?" I asked. I was so perplexed by this explanation because we got tickets to pick up our soap monthly. But this company had to sell soap! "Their soap is not distributed out?"

"Well, yes, they distribute it through selling, not tickets. The company needs to sell their soap, or they will be out of business."

"Out of business? You mean they are in the business of selling soap?" I did not understand the word business at that time. How could anyone sell what should be given away? I was so lost.

Everything we got with tickets was so scarce. Sometimes, even if you had a ticket, the merchant would run out. If we used all of our soap before the end of the month, we could not buy more. We had to wait for the next month and another ticket to get more soap.

"Why advertise soap when there is never enough soap?" I wondered. This was crazy. I did not know about supply and demand. In school, our teacher told us that the capitalist countries would pour milk into the ocean instead of giving it to people. It was beyond my comprehension; so my emotion towards capitalist countries was nothing but hatred.

Soap, milk, advertising, and business would not make sense to me for many more years.

A Bigger World

I never understood poverty when I was in China. I considered my childhood to be a very sweet one. To combat being poor, my mom told me that I looked at my best when I wore my sister's old clothes. I believed her and was never dissatisfied with anything I put on myself.

My world was very small and contained, but very pleasant. I was like a fish in a bowl which would never question the quality of the water. If I ever showed any tendency to admire others' wealth, my parents would tell me in unison, "Money is dirty, and making it is even worse. Learning knowledge is the ultimate way of living; so go back to study and be good at school," they would say.

They were both well-educated people making a minimum wage. My mother was an engineer, and my father a professor. Despite their low wage, their work was honorable compared to anything commercial.

You can understand why, in the 60s and 70s, the concept of business was never present. It was outside the realm of my imagination. I just did not know what it meant.

In the early 1980s, China had already begun its free-market initiatives. At that time, wealth started to show up on the street. I would meet people who were just like me but incredibly wealthy, and they were all from overseas. They displayed wealth in a way that I was completely unable to imagine.

I began to realize that the world outside my home was larger and more different than I had understood. I started to think of leaving this fishbowl.

On the surface, the wealthy world seemed somewhat related to the English language, as if speaking English would bring me a better life. So I decided to pursue English school in Toronto, Canada, where our family had many relatives living.

Something You Cannot Do

On the fateful day of January 15, 1989, I landed at Toronto International Airport. I did not sleep at all during the 14-hour flight from China, and I also did not eat, as my stomach had a knot. With nothing more than two cardboard boxes and a phone number, I pushed myself out of customs as a foreign student at York University.

A kid from a communist country had landed in the capitalist world. Because I knew how to share naturally, I was a very pleasant person to others, but I had nothing to share. I made friends, but I could not keep them because of my poverty.

I did not even have 25 cents to make a call to tell my friends that

I would be late to meet them. Of course, I would be late, as I had no car. Too embarrassed to tell anyone how poor I was, I never shared rides with friends. I would meet them wherever we were going. It is not easy to meet anyone on time when you are on foot most of the time.

I knew that school would change my life and help me get a good job. So I needed to come up with money to go to school. Someone told me to start a business. They also told me that being a bartender was almost like having a business because I could make a lot of cash.

So I searched the *Toronto Star* up and down looking for a bartender position in a close by area. I found one and called. "Hi, this is Ying, and I like to apply for the bartender position."

The person on the other end paused a bit too long. Maybe she was struggling with my accent. "Do you even know what a bartender does?" The person on the other line could tell I was new to this world.

But I needed this job. So even though I did not know, I said, "Yeah, I know, just tending the bar."

The person on the phone had heard enough. "It is not something you can do." Click. She cut me off.

It was so hard for me to be told, "It is not something you can do!" Those words echoed in my heart for years.

BEING INDEPENDENT

Meanwhile, my financial status was growing worse. I ran out of money to pay rent. Out of desperation, I asked my roommates who shared the floor with me, "Can I clean for you both, to exchange for this month rent?"

There was a long pause; both of them looked at me as if I was crazy. Finally, one of them said softly, "Are you out of your mind?"

I moved out. This was the fourth time moving out during my first three months in Toronto. I first lived with my aunt. Too scared to move out, I was a squatter; then I moved to a place as a live-in nanny for a couple of weeks. I made $300 on babysitting while living rent-free; then I rented a room in a friend's home until I found out that her husband really was more interested in me than my rent. I moved again to this place with two other girls near the school. Now it was gone.

Yes, I was young and beautiful (if I do say so myself). My biggest dream was to marry someone who could rescue me from poverty. I waited and I tried and I failed. So I knew I had to make it on my own.

The toughness of life, the unforgiving pain of lacking, the deep shame of wanting … all of that hurt and longing was the energy in me that enabled me to move forward. I thought about starting a business every day.

Thirty years later, looking back, I see that knowledge about doing business was hardly the reason for me to start my own business. Knowledge alone would not see me through the hard work that is necessary to get a business going. No, I had to rely on that strong desire.

And even that strong desire would need to be guided by my choices as an immigrant from the Country of the Heart, someone who needed to help and serve other people. I found that out the hard way! I will tell you that story a little later.

UNEXPECTED BUSINESS

Someone I admire who is an immigrant from the Country of the Heart is Eckhart Tolle. Like me, he draws energy and satisfaction from helping other people. Like me, his first thought was not starting a business. And like me, too, he is an immigrant - from Germany to Canada.

Being fellow Canadians as well as fellow Heart people makes me feel very close to Eckhart Tolle!

You may not think of Tolle as someone who is a businessman,

because he is well-known as a spiritual leader. However, he is the head of a business that sells books and other materials and conducts seminars and retreats. The things that he makes cost money; so he is a businessman.

How did someone so spiritual and so concerned with the welfare of others come to start a business?

I am sure that if I asked Eckhart Tolle in person, "Why did you start this business?" he would say something like, "I did not plan to start a business; I only wanted to fill a need." That is the answer of a Heart person!

In 1995, Tolle moved to the west coast of Canada, where he saw spiritual freedom in the people. He published *The Power of Now* in 1997. Three years later, Oprah recommended it to her audience, and Tolle sold millions.[1]

Gradually, this small published book grew to become a wellness empire. Many people work with Tolle now, making and distributing his materials and helping with his conferences. Those people have jobs because Tolle has been listening to what people want from him and meeting their needs. He is not inventing things and persuading people to want them with advertising tricks. No – he is filling real needs in the world.

People have asked Tolle whether making money is something a spiritual person can do. He told them that focusing on money is not something a spiritual person can do. But spiritual people can do things that they enjoy and that contribute to the world. The universe tends to reward joy and contribution. If money comes your way from doing these things, then you can enjoy it, as long as you do not form attachment to it.[2] Your motive is all that matters.

THE BURN LEVEL IN YOUR HANDS

However, not all business owners come from the Country of the Heart, and that is all right. Some of the clients I really love come from the Country of the Hand. They are focused on the outcome of the product; they believe that if the product is good enough, the rest of the business challenges will fall into place naturally. They are loyal, creative people who work hard physically and mentally.

JOSE'S BIRTHDAY

I see my own strong energy in my client Jose, who runs a farm equipment repair shop with more than 10 employees working for him. He also is one of my very long-time clients.

I have watched him start, expand, and excel in business for the past 20 years. He has remained such a steady, successful client of mine that I will be using his example in future books. When I asked him why he was in business, without much thinking, he said, "I wished I could work as an employee. I would work hard for my boss, and I would be a good employee. But I did not have a social security number. I had to make it on my own."

Jose was born in a small town in the northern part of Mexico. Ever since he was little, he would hear stories about how the brave man would go through the rugged mountains and cross a winding river to arrive in the United States and work there to make a lot of money. He had made up his mind that he would go to the USA on his 25th birthday with his wife and his 1-year-old son.

To travel so far for work is regarded as a heroic spirit in his village. Away back home, people told him that he can find a job easily and that, once he settles in, his boy can go to American school for free. The school bus would even drive the kids to school! No walking. That news made him smile, as he had gone to his school walking on bare feet 4 miles each day for 7 years.

But here, somehow, he was condemned for coming so far to work. He did not understand this immigration visa and immigration status thing. He did not know that in the USA he would be called "undocumented" or "illegal" for the action he took to pursue his happiness.

Jose failed to find a job, as every employer he met was asking him to provide W-4 and I-9 forms. These forms would ask him for his social security number. He learned that he did not have one, and his wife and his boy would not have one either.

So he gave up on his hope of working for an employer and started to do things for people directly. Starting a business for him wasn't a choice. It was a need. And he did what he knew how to do and what he liked to do. Focusing on the work at hand instead of pleasing clients or winning the game of making money shows me that although Jose is from Mexico, he is really a business immigrant from the Country of the Hand.

ELON'S DREAMS

Though he is worlds apart in experience from Jose, another person from the Country of the Hand is someone I admire very much: Elon Musk.

Musk came to Canada for college, just as I did, and then he emigrated to the USA, where he saw a lot of opportunity. He moved to Silicon Valley and decided not to study for his doctorate. Instead he started an Internet company called Zip2 with his brother. This company was like an early version of Google Maps plus the Yellow Pages. Musk saw a lot of possibility in the Internet, and he wanted to maximize it.[3]

That desire was one stepping stone on the way to making amazing things: building electric cars, maximizing solar power, and helping humans travel in space. Those products had formed part of his dreams since he was a child. Starting his first business was the way Musk saw that he could do work he loved and reach his dreams.[4]

Here is where the burn level happened for Elon Musk. He knew the products he wanted to make. He knew what he wanted them to do and the change he wanted them to make in the world.

No other company was doing what Elon wanted to do. No other business existed that would let him make what he wanted to make. So his only option was to start his own business. That was his only choice.

His burn level would not be ignored.

Someone that focused on the work in front of him has to be from the Country of the Hand! And someone that desperate to start making his own products definitely has the right burn level to start a business. If you are thinking about starting a business, think about whether you are determined to make one kind of thing. Maybe you are from the Country of the Hand like Elon Musk.

THE BURN LEVEL IN YOUR HEAD

The third type of clients that I see have a passport from the Country of the Head. The client with this passport is concerned with making money and being a success more than anything else. And someone I admire as a businessperson who is definitely from the Country of the Head is Donald Trump. As a business owner, he can teach us a lot.

SOMETHING MORE

Many people do not know that Donald Trump's mother was an immigrant from the UK. His father was the son of immigrants from Sweden. And he is married to a lady who emigrated from Slovenia. The mother of his older children came from Czechoslovakia. So Donald Trump's story begins as an immigrant's story.

His father, Fred Trump, built housing developments in Queens, New York, but Donald wanted to do more. So he went to the Wharton School of Business (same college where Elon Musk got his degree) and started doing big real estate deals in Manhattan.[5]

And here is what tells me, even more than that ambitious decision, that Donald Trump is from the Country of the Head. He says at the very beginning of *The Art of the Deal,* "Deals are my art form. Other people paint beautifully on canvas or write wonderful poetry. I like making deals, preferably big deals. That's how I get my kicks."[6]

You see? Only someone from the Country of the Head could say something like that!

Lady in Mink

Another client of mine, Emily, is a red-haired, city-bred lady and a true Iowan. She is someone I know for sure is from the Country of the Head. I could tell at first sight that she would not have the same kind of need to start a business as Jose did. But looks don't always tell the truth about the determination in your heart.

I remember that the first time I met her, Emily was wearing a white mink coat. She opened my office's front door, just about to walk in, when an Asian man was about to go out. He was wearing blue overalls with white paint dripped all over his outfit; he had just picked up some payroll checks and was leaving. They literally met at the door and passed each other so close that I thought their outfits touched. That would have been too bad for the mink coat!

I quickly got up from my desk and jokingly said, "Looks like I need to make this door bigger!"

Emily looked at me and said, "Are you Ying Sa?"

"Yes," I smiled at her.

She did not even try to look at me. While taking off her expensive mink coat, she said, "My friend told me that you have a lot of people coming to see you, but I did not realize I would have to fight my way through this door!"

That was our first encounter. She had come to see me about her taxes. At that time, Emily held a full-time job as an executive secretary for one of the partners at a well-known local law firm. This partner to whom she reported was a crazy old man, and she was never comfortable with his gaze. "He would look at me as if

I was stupid; you know what he is thinking."

Emily complained about her boss: "You wonder why these law firms only have bald-headed old men? What happened to the smart and good-looking ladies?"

I could not help but chuckle when she said that. She had her hands on her hips, her chin up, and just that movie star posture – a perfect professional. She met a lot of businesspeople at her job, and sometimes she even got to see clients' business books and records. Seeing those records encouraged her that she could do the same thing if she had the time.

One day, Emily made an appointment with me because she wanted to quit her job and start her own business. She wanted my firm to assist her in setting up a business entity, applying for a license to operate, and reviewing some business documents. For her own business, she struggled with what to do, but starting a business so she could get away from the boss and use her smarts full time, that was a done deal.

On and off she settled on opening a restaurant. She did not know anything about running a restaurant other than the fact that everyone she knew made money in doing it. I stared at her perfectly polished French tip nails and wondered whether she could handle the physical hard work.

But her voice rang with sincerity. "I am tired of working 8-5 at this place. I actually would love to work more. Oh well, my boss is so cheap, and he does not want me to work overtime. I want to be my own boss. My friend will cook. I am doing it."

Emily was only in her 40s. According to her, her life was just about to start, and it was time to gamble. That willingness to gamble on herself told me that Emily was from the Country of the Head! Her husband also had a full-time job that paid well, and he promised her that he would help keep the food on the table in case she failed the business.

She was determined to go through with the business, although I felt bad about her good job. Emily had a good life, but not fulfilling enough for her to call it good.

THE CHEESE GAMBLE

I have another client, Tony, who worked at a good job for many years and saved half a million dollars in his 401K plan by age 59. He could work a couple of more years to retire from his position. Instead he was planning to gamble his half a million 401K.

"Ying, I want to put my retirement savings into a cheese factory."

"A brand-new factory?" I asked.

He leaned back in his chair. "Yes, from scratch. For a kind of cheese that only I know how to do. You cannot get it easily here. I want to invest in the factory; I want to start it now."

"At your age, to gamble on all your retirement savings? That is crazy!"

"Maybe so," Tony said. "I have some experience in this industry. I did the math. I will sell it to make money, probably not run it to make money."

I was scared for Tony to lose everything he had worked so hard to save. For me, a factory like that would not have been a good investment for a 60-year-old. But Tony was willing to gamble on the chance of success. So he made the investment.

Ten years later at age 70, Tony sold his company for $24 million! He retired for the second time, but this time with a lot more than half a million. His gamble paid off!

And the fact that he calculated his risk and he sold the factory without any feeling attachment tells me that he is a Head person.

NOT BACKGROUND BUT BURN LEVEL

Obviously, what is good for one person is not the same as what is good for another. Jose would love to be able to work like Emily does, but his circumstances and his inner desires to take care of his family directed him in his path. Emily wanted freedom and profit. I wanted a good living and to make people happy.

In the same way, what makes sense to Donald Trump does not

make sense to Elon Musk or Eckhart Tolle. We are all different. We come to life assuming different things are true and expecting different things to happen. None of those things are 100% accurate when we come to the Land of Business.

Well, everyone has their own reasons for wanting to do a business.

There are clients of mine who get into business because they got laid off. Or they thought of a good idea that warrants a successful business. Or their parents died and left the struggling kids to take over the business. There are different outer situations, and there are different inner desires.

People with the same situations look at them in different ways, depending on what "passport" they hold. Whether they are from the Country of the Hand, the Country of the Heart, or the Country of the Head. The reality is that, like all business immigrants, you can be successful if you are conscious of your nationality when you enter the Land of Business and at the same time you have the Burn.

This is the principle my clients taught me: You do not need to have any business experience to begin a business. You just need to have that burn inside and to be aware of your type of "passport."

REFLECTION #1 WHAT IS YOUR PASSPORT?

What passport do you hold? Maybe you already know. If you don't, then answer the questions below.

Here are the rules: 1) Do not think too deeply about your answers, 2) Do not answer each question according to how you wish you would respond, and 3) Answer each question according to how you know you have normally responded in the past.

Your answers will help you understand if you are from the Country of the Hand, the Heart, or the Head.

If you answer honestly, your passport choice will let you know all the possibilities that could cause your business endeavors to win or to fail:

	SCENARIOS
1	**How you take advantage of a time-sensitive opportunity.** A. Consult the advice of someone close to you. B. Check your calendar. C. Take the opportunity and work out the details later.
2	**How you prepare for an interview.** A. Get the format and practice your answers. B. Be spontaneous or "wing it." C. Research the person who will be interviewing you.
3	**How you persuade someone to see things your way.** A. Put pressure on them by threatening with consequences. B. Make a reasonable argument and explain it point by point. C. Paint as positive a picture as you can for your side.
4	**What you do when you are overwhelmed** A. Drop everything and take a break until you feel better. B. Write out a list of things that you need to do. C. Call someone up and ask them for help.
5	**How you determine that someone is innocent.** A. Believe him or her. B. Watch him or her carefully and quietly. C. Ask him or her.
6	**How you determine if something is going to be a problem.** A. You see something little or odd that seems out of place. B. You won't really know until it becomes obvious. C. You are never surprised at anything..
7	**How you start a conversation with someone you don't know.** A. Lok for something that you have in common. B. Talk about unimportant things. C. Talk about important things.

8	**How you get in contact with someone who is hard to reach.** A. Make an appointment. B. Keep calling until they pick up. C. Wait for the right time.
9	**What you do when someone owes you money.** A. Remind them periodically when you see them. B. Mail them an invoice. C. Give them lots of time or eventually forget it.
10	**How you remember complicated information.** A. Memorize it. B. Rmember the main points and then connect the dots. C. Put it in the form of a story.
11	**How your mind works.** A. Like a spiderweb: things just stick to it. B. Like a machine: pretty much the same way for everything. C. Like radar: it zeroes in on what it thinks is important.
12	**How you teach others best.** A. Isolate a problem much like a judge. B. Demonstrate or act out the problem. C. Explain the problem in detail.
13	**How you make sure that someone understands you.** A. Repeat everything. B. Ask if they have any questions. C. Assume that they understand.
14	**How you design your office/workspace.** A. To reflect your style and personality. B. To be a productive place. C. To be like other offices/workspaces.

15	**How you influence people.** A. You bring energy and enthusiasm. B. You bring conscience and logic. C. You bring something that people find very practical.
16	**How you defend someone who has done no wrong.** A. Mention the good that they do. B. Reprimand the offender. C. Change the subject.
17	**How you apologize.** A. Do something nice with no words. B. Offer one formal apology C. Apologize over and over again.

To check your answers,
go to Appendix 1 at the end of the book.

REFLECTION #2: WHAT IS YOUR BURN LEVEL?

Read the statements that follow the diagram below and ask yourself the question, "Do I have the burn? And, if so, then what level?" Rate your answers to these statements from 1 to 10. 1-3 (SPARK), 4-6 (FLAME), and 7-10 (BLAZE). Use the rating system below.

BURN LEVEL RATING SYSTEM			
Measure	*SPARK*	*FLAME*	*BLAZE*
Low	1	4	7
Medium	2	5	8
High	3	6	9-10

1. How many times in a day do you think about starting a business?
2. Are you afraid to start a business?
3. Are you jealous of any of your friends who are in business for themselves?

46

3. Do people tend to come to you for a product or service you have not monetized (like a recipe or advice, etc.)?

4. In the last 30 days, have you made money outside your regular work?

To calculate your burn level, add your answers. You have The Burn if your score is 19 or higher. The higher your burn level, the more pain you are experiencing in your daily life. So what is your burn level?

Here is what I tell my clients: The burn level is the reflection of your current life situation. There is no good or bad, right or wrong about being on a certain burn level. You might even change your burn level if you take this test a year later. However if you do have a high burn level, you need to study this book. You only have one life, and you happen to be living in this great nation: the USA. What are you waiting for?

Appointment with Ying @ 8am

Chapter 2

What Business Would Fit Me?

ONLY YOU CAN ANSWER

There are many questions in business that a professional can help to answer. But not this one. Answering the question of what business will suit you is truly a journey to self-discovery.

The reflections for the first chapter can put you on the path to discovering who you really are in relation to getting into a business: in other words, what language you would speak when you are facing a danger – your gut reaction. *Reflection #1* is like a culture test.

You need to know if you are from the Country of the Hand, the Country of the Heart, or the Country of the Head. If you know already which country you are from, then you know which passport you hold. With that understanding, that passport, now you will be able to focus on the appropriate sections in the rest of the book.

In Reflection 2, we want you to have a way to calculate your burn level. Do you know what your burn level is? How motivated are you to start a business right now? Should you wait and learn first, or is the time right today?

The questions of what burn level motivates you and what kind of passport you carry are questions only you can answer. And I want you to answer them! I am a big believer in early planning.

At Community CPA, we offer tax planning. Most traditional CPA firms calculate only the past; they announce what already happened to their clients with a historian-like approach. At Community CPA, we look at the passport our client holds, and we implement strategy based on client culture. We analyze the data, and for folks with a passport from the Country of the Head, we will plan a strong balance sheet so the business can be sold whenever the money is on the table. We are not historians; we are planners.

Every November, we organize a tax planning session with our clients. We calculate the year ahead of December 31, and we make tax and accounting implementations before the year ends. Many of our clients care more about meeting us in November than on April 15!

So planning and asking the right questions are essential to running a good business. In the same way, the question of how you will find what business to do depends on the kind of passport you hold. People from the countries of the Hand, Heart, and Head start different businesses for reasons that relate to different cultural backgrounds. Maybe the stories in this chapter will help you think about what motivates you.

WHAT IS THE WORK IN FRONT OF YOU?

Do you remember my client Jose? He did not know what he could do when he had just gotten off the freight train with his wife and his small son.

Jose's First Job

It was 3am, and he was hungry. His wife Maria, who was still breastfeeding Junior, was looking pale under the streetlight. Cars went by really fast. They seemed to drive a lot faster than they did where he came from. He was a bit shaky to cross the highway.

They walked along the hills perpendicular to the highway, and soon the morning got brighter. The sound of the highway was gone.

Jose and his family stopped in front of a small house where the grass was tall and saw that one window in front of the house was open. Jose took a deep breath and knocked. An old lady opened the door.

She looked at him, and she also noticed his wife holding the baby. The old lady pointed at the chairs in front of her house, signaling for Maria to sit. Negotiating with broken English, Jose arranged to mow the yard and got $5.00 for the work. Just before the little family left, the old lady gave Jose two more bills - $10.00 each.

He had done his first American job.

PRACTICAL EDUCATION

Along the way to Iowa, Jose worked on houses that had over-grown grass. Because he did not have his own mower, he often ended up fixing the machines at the owner's home. By the time he finally arrived in Davenport, Iowa, he had already learned the inner workings of some brand-name lawn mowers, like Honda, EGO, and even a riding lawn mower by John Deere.

When I asked him about whether he went to school to learn mechanics, he shook his head so fast that I felt dizzy. He told me that as long as he had his hands on a machine, he knew what to do for it. That is the answer of someone from the Country of the Hand.

For Jose, the choice of what to do for a business wasn't so much a choice as a happy accident. The work he saw to do was mowing lawns and fixing lawnmowers. He didn't have to do much soul searching about what talents and desires he had.

Jose's experience with deciding on a business reminds me that he is coming to the Land of Business from the Country of the Hand. He has a talent and knowledge that he uses to do work. He is not focused on giving back to clients or maximizing profits with a smart business strategy.

BUILDING PRODUCTS TO SAVE THE WORLD

The way Jose decided on a business is like the way Elon Musk decided on a business. Musk had a deep, inner desire to make products to support the industries of the Internet, electric cars, solar energy, and space travel. When he sold his first company, Zip2, to Compaq for $307 million, he earned $22 million for himself.[7] He would never have to work again. But he chose to keep working and build companies because he wanted to make things that interested him.

He had not finished with maximizing the Internet. His new virtual product was to build an Internet bank. Now, many people use PayPal. But when Musk started X.com, which soon merged with PayPal, his kind of bank was brand new. People had run banks the same way for hundreds of years. To make an Internet bank was something people had not done before.[8]

To start X.com, Musk hired people from the worlds of banking and computers. Ed Fricker, who came from a Canadian bank, did not like the way Musk ran the company. He left, taking many of the employees with him. The company nearly folded, even though Musk had put $12 million of his own money into it.

But Musk did not give up. He got the licenses he needed, hired new workers, and he invented new financial products. X.com did not charge fees for its bank accounts, and it gave people money for signing up. That seemed backwards! One of the new product features Musk made was the ability for people to pay each other directly instead of waiting days and days for a bank computer. When his bank opened to the public, it was a success.[9]

Elon Musk invents products at an instinct level. What he does, he does because he is devoted to that work. He has said, "Maybe I read too many comics as a kid. In the comics, it always seems like they are trying to save the world. It seemed like one should try to make the world a better place because the inverse makes no sense."

If you look at what Musk does, it looks like he is trying to save the world, just like a hero in a comic book. Solar power and electric cars – these are future technologies that some advanced people should have, but Musk wants them now. Sending humans to Mars so that one tragedy will not kill all of us – this, too, is something a comic book hero would do. You can look at the little boy Musk and look at the grown-up Musk and see the same burn inside.

The desire to make the future now and to save the world with his wonderful products are deep inner desires for Elon Musk. Musk does not start the latest, most fashionable businesses. He does not do something the public is asking him to do. And he has almost lost many fortunes in making what he wants to make.

That is okay with him, because what he is doing comes from who he is.

WHAT DO OTHER PEOPLE NEED FROM YOU?

For me, someone from the Country of the Heart, I struggled with finding what I liked to do in my twenties. I am definitely not the kind of person who knows what I want from the get-go. Originally, I wanted to study law, but my English was so limited at the time that the law school would not consider me.

The only school that accepted me was a business school's accounting program. The whole time in school, I was working at Bank of America as an accounting clerk doing bank reconciliation for some bank accounts. I did not understand the function of my job at the time. I just knew that being an accountant really sucked.

Mall Tax

I wanted to start a business and do something different, but I was not good at anything. Well, I take that back. I loved art, and I was pretty good with making dried flower wreaths and creative clay earrings.

I discovered my talent. So after graduating with my accounting degree, I started doing something I was good at. I quit my Bank of America job, rented a cart in the mall, and started to make these art pieces while tending the booth.

I spent 18 hours a day standing, making, and selling. In my first month, I made $758.00 gross sales. After paying the $750 monthly rent, I was left with $8.00, which did not cover my $5,800 material expenses. Riding on the subway going back to my apartment, I could not stop tears coming down my cheeks. I loved what I was doing. Why wasn't I making money doing it?

The next day, a new month was starting. I could not cancel my lease; so I knew that I must keep on going. Two Filipino ladies came by, and we started talking. They were impressed with my artwork, but they were even more surprised by my accounting and business degree from York University.

They said, "Wow, we have some tax issues right now. Would you please help us? We will buy some earrings from you."

They came back with the tax documents, and within a week, I fixed the issue. Next thing I knew, I started to do accounting and tax work for people who came by my cart. I had some income from helping on taxes, and for the first time, I felt that I could make my rent and have some money left over. However, most of the sales came from my accounting work, not from selling my artwork.

Not a Bean Counter!

I struggled with reality. I hated being an accountant. I couldn't be known as a bean counter! I was pretty and sexy, not a dreaded accountant wearing thick glasses and buried under big piles of papers. That was not me. But I had just made a profit for the first time! What was I going to do?

Soon the mall manager came by my cart. I thought he was there to congratulate me, because when I paid my rent for the month, I smiled instead of crying. But that wasn't the case.

He stood next to me, waited for one of my accounting clients to leave, and said, "Ying, your lease agreement with us is to do flower arrangements and handmade crafts. You cannot do tax and accounting services, as we already have a tenant who does that. You are in violation of your lease terms with us. I am afraid you have to go."

I felt sick to my stomach. This "violation of lease terms" was such a scary phrase and sounded so illegal that I felt like I was going to faint. As you can expect, I lost my spot at the mall.

All the materials I purchased and all the earrings I made, I simply wasted them all. Defeated completely, I started to look for a job – a real job that could pay for my losses. And it was becoming clear what that real job was going to be.

It wasn't just the fact that the accounting work made money and the artwork did not. What was pulling me in the direction of working with taxes and balance sheets was people. With my artwork, I pleased myself. With my accounting, I pleased others.

My clients needed me, and they appreciated me. Their willingness to pay my fees was just one kind of evidence that I was doing something good for them. That makes a real difference for a Heart person!

Satisfaction

Before long, the two Filipino ladies called. They were so excited to find me, as they had friends who needed my help urgently. Their business had gotten audited by Revenue Canada.

One of the ladies urged me, "Please help, and our friend will pay you. We told him how smart you are and how you helped us."

I decided to take a look at the case. Revenue Canada had assessed unreported income of this business based on Revenue Canada's imagination of the lifestyle of a business owner who would spend $20,000 or more on vacation alone each year and regularly buy luxuries. The tax owed amount was over $50,000, a number that I had never, ever seen in my short years of Canadian life. I took the case as I knew, from my personal experience, that the Revenue-Canada-imagined lifestyle of a business owner does not apply to many, many small business owners.

A year later, I won the case, and the tax amount was completely eliminated. The adrenalin of winning kept me on a high note, and I loved it. The more accounting I did, the more confidence I gained from doing it. I started to think, "Maybe I am really good at this thing that I do not like to do."

I found my talent through the satisfaction of my clients. I did not discover my talent on my own. Others who worked with me shone the spotlight on my talent, and a business venture was born without my mind designing it first. I found a way to help people and make them happy. That made me love my work!

Asking for Happiness

That is the same thing that happened with Eckhart Tolle! In 1977 when Tolle was studying for his doctorate at Cambridge University, he experienced a spiritual change. He was so depressed, and he thought of killing himself. But at that moment, he found the truth. His ego burned away in a single night. Amazing!

For a few years, Tolle just enjoyed being. He did not even work regularly. After his inner transformation happened, he wandered around Cambridge for years, just being happy within himself. He was not concerned with finding work or starting anything new.

Then people from Cambridge asked about his peacefulness. Eckhart taught them and others. It was not until people found him and asked him about the difference in his life that he began teaching.

That was a perfect start for a Heart person! Other people told Tolle what they needed from him, and he was happy to offer it to them. His understanding brought him joy. Helping other people gain understanding also brought him joy. He listened to others to find out what job he should do.[11]

WHERE DO YOU FIND SUCCESS?

If you are a person from the Country of the Head, then you may recognize in yourself the feeling of ambition. You want to do something big, which pretty much means big money. What other people have done before you is not valuable to you when you see that you can do something greater.

Cincinnati Success

When Donald Trump graduated from college, he could have gone to work at his father's company under his father's direction. Fred Trump was building housing units in Brooklyn and Queens, managing them, and collecting the rent. That was a steady business.

But Donald Trump wanted something more for himself. He heard about a government subsidized housing complex in Cincinnati, Ohio that was in trouble. Residents were damaging the apartments and not paying rent.

The complex was not a pretty place, but Trump saw an opportunity. He convinced his father to help him buy the place. Then he evicted the non-paying residents, landscaped the grounds, fixed the apartments and made them beautiful, and then began filling them with new clients who could pay the rent.

However, almost as soon as the apartments were finished and full, the neighborhood around them began to turn bad. Trump knew that his investment would not stay good long. Before residents could terminate their leases, Trump sold the whole development to a real estate investment trust for a profit.[12]

Trump was willing to change course from his father's business to make money. He was willing to experiment with a new kind of real estate. He was also willing to walk away when money was on the line. He found that he was good at identifying profit opportunities in distressed property and making the most money fast.

Too Many Cooks

Many of my clients may have started a business for one thing, but the business turned itself into something else. In the end though, the original intention wasn't really important. Making money was what counted.

A similar thing happened to my client Emily with her restaurant business. A determined person, she came to me literally weekly. At one appointment, I sat looking at her with some amusement.

For the past three weeks, we had cut four final paychecks for four chefs she had fired. She was changing chefs like a baby changes diapers. "What, you got another one?" I teased her.

"Yeah, I know," she smiled. "I'm sorry; I cannot put up with them. I have to let them go."

I pictured a long line of chefs in white hats and jackets waiting outside Emily's restaurant and going through a revolving door one by one. "Where do you get all these chefs lined up for you to pick? The other restaurants are struggling to find anyone to cook!"

"I have connections, and I have a lot of them to pick from," she answered.

About six months later, Emily closed the restaurant and turned the restaurant location into a manpower agency for restaurateurs. She used the kitchen to train new employees for clients.

She said to me, "I thought running a restaurant would be easy money; well, I guess this is still like running the restaurant. You see, I don't need to deal with bad cooks anymore, and I make better money."

Emily lost all her savings in the restaurant business venture. But she landed on something related to it and started to make it. She was gifted in making connections; with her beauty and charm and her high-school-level Spanish she became one of the biggest job agencies for local restaurateurs.

Power and Money

She said to me, "I thought I would work less and make more when I quit my job, but I am actually making less and working more now. Well, I really enjoy bossing myself around!"

"Oh really? Are you happy to get paid less and work more?" I looked at her with a smile.

"Yeah, at my business everyone thinks I am smart and magic; well, I was not that smart when I was working in the law office," she sighed. "If only I knew I would work for less and work more for my own business, I would have stayed at my nice job. But it's okay. I learned a lot from my restaurant. I think I really enjoy my work now; so I don't really care about my hours or my pay."

As one successful business owner says, "I've consistently learned from my mistakes, and to me, even if they're costly -- and some of them have been – if I learn something new, I consider it a positive experience."[13] For Emily, the satisfaction of having power over her own life meant more to her than money. That was something her old boss at the law firm couldn't have given her, no matter how many raises he approved.

The nature of her law office job did not allow her to be loud and hyper energetic. The soft little voice that she had to utter on the phone was like a silly game; she wanted to laugh loudly and speak loudly. She did not care about her mink coat anymore, as that was only for that kind of work.

She found her true nature with this "less pay but more work" kind of job. Power to be herself and do as she pleased satisfied Emily. And she trusted herself to make lots of money at her business once she learned the ins and outs.

Money was still a game to Emily, and she knew more was coming. The power to make it was in her own being.

Later Emily wrote a blog in a local newspaper. The title was: "Learn Yourself. Discovering Your Talents and Desires Is a Journey."

FINDING A BUSINESS IS PERSONAL

For some people, the confirmation of your talent comes from outside you. An encouraging word, a smile, and a "No Change Letter" from Revenue Canada guided me in my search. I never believed that I would be a bean counter. But with the success I achieved in my clients' cases, I was counting beans happily because I felt needed and appreciated.

Luck Finds Me

I immigrated to Des Moines, Iowa from Toronto, Canada in 1996. The vast difference in immigrant population between these two cities made me believe that my family was the only minority family in this whole state. At the playground in front of our apartment building, one little girl held my daughter's little face and marveled: "Look, a China doll!"

Her observation was followed by my daughter's loud cry. Lulu had just turned two at that time, and she never was treated this way in Toronto. But here in the middle of Iowa, she was visibly special.

I felt minoritized once again, not in a negative way, just like my Mongolian-ethnic family was in China.

Soon I discovered those who were just like me. Soon I discovered the needs of immigrants who owned businesses in the state.

In the year 1997, I was employed at Iowa State University as the CFO for Iowa Manufacturing Extension Partnership. The nameplate on the wall indicated: Chief Financial Officer, Ying Sa.

One night while I was working late, the custodian in the building came to me. "Your name is Ying?" He pointed at my nameplate and said: "You know IRS?"

I was going to say no because I really did not know much about the IRS, but he had already handed over a letter for me to read. It was a letter from the Internal Revenue Service. I thought to myself, "This is where I will be filing my own tax this year."

The custodian's name was Luck Nguyen. Luck continued: "I did not know what happened to tax. IRS wanted more money from me; me has no more money. Can you call for me? No English for me."

I agreed and learned that he was a Vietnamese immigrant. I was apparently the only Asian he knew who could read English. To him, the word financial on my plate meant that I must be someone who has a lot of knowledge in money and could talk to the IRS. I took the letter quickly and promised him that I would get back to him tomorrow night at this time.

The next night, he came. I told him that the IRS was going to refund him $680, as he overpaid his taxes. The letter was to tell him that and to notify him that he should get the check in the mail in about two weeks' time. With the letter date, I told him he should be getting his check in the next two days.

He did not fully believe what I said, and maybe he did not understand my English. Anyway, he left without much expression, and I thought he was disappointed.

Three days passed, and I forgot about Luck and the IRS. Then he showed up bright and early and knocked on my door. Without any words, he showed me the IRS check. He pointed at the sky and said: "You are God send. You are good!"

That night I had about five people coming to see me, all immigrants, and we set up appointments to discuss their cases individually at my home office. All of them had issues with government notices, some of which were three years old.

Starting with Luck the custodian, the Universe started to send me business.

DEEP DESIRES

So what spoke to me inside is knowing I was needed by others. That is also what appealed to Eckhart Tolle. That quality is so ordinary, yet used properly, it is extraordinary. If you are like me, a Heart person, then look to what you can do to make people happy, and you will find your business.

But maybe you are different. Sometimes you just know in your gut what you are good at doing. The talent you find within yourself does not need to be big or amazing or unique. Those little things in life that you repeatedly offer others become your skill and your talent.

When you are like Jose, you just know what to do because you can fix anything and everything. Maybe you need to think about what comes easily to you. Maybe you are like Elon Musk, and you have an inner drive to create important products. If you are like Jose or Elon, a Hand person, look at the work you are passionate about doing to find your business.

If you are like Emily, you may find what you are good at doing through trial and error. Emily is good at training and networking, and she found out that quality of hers through her failure in business. She wasn't hung up on doing a restaurant. She wanted freedom and profit, and she was willing to change and experiment to get what she wanted.

Maybe you just need to get started and fine-tune the details later, like she did. Maybe you need to try something new, like Donald Trump did when he was starting out. If you are a Head person, then you will understand taking a risk. You will value the end result when your business is making money.

Whatever way you arrive at the knowledge of what kind of business you should start, you are the only person who can know for sure what business would best fit you. No one else can decide for you, though other people can give you input about what they see in you. Listen to them, but understand that only you know what is in your head, your heart, and your hands.

REFLECTION #3: DISCOVER YOURSELF

For the next five days, write down what you were doing at the following moments:

	DISCOVERING YOURSELF	
1	*Your heart was just happy – maybe you saw something or someone that made you happy. It could be anything; just be honest about why at that moment you smiled.*	
2	*You were wondering why something you were doing could be so hard for others but easy for you – for example, your colleague failed to finish his work again and you had to help. Write down what that was.*	
3	*Notice any time that you said to yourself, "I wish I could just do this forever." What was that?*	
4	*Notice when you forgot about meals because you were merged into something that you liked and felt it was important to finish.*	
	TOTAL POINTS>>	

You might say, "None of the above, and my only happy time for the past five days was drinking and eating." If that is healthy, then you might have a passion for that experience. If you say, "I noticed that I am good at talking to folks when they are down," then maybe your talent is in the self-help industry.

For each of the four items, if you actually found the incidents for every item, you can give 25 points to each item. If you have fewer than 50 points, I would not start any business at this point but join (or continue in) the workforce to discover yourself while working.

If your score is higher than 50, then you know you have a passion and know what kind of business fits you.

REFLECTION #4: THE CHILDHOOD THEME TEST

Elon Musk has built many businesses based on the nature of the product that he wanted to build as a child reading comic books. Donald Trump built a real estate empire on the foundation of the work he saw his father doing when he was a little boy. And Eckhart Tolle spent an unhappy childhood around parents who were miserable in their own lives, and then he found joy as a man spreading a message of inner peace and contentment.

Think about your own childhood, and answer the following questions:

	CHILDHOOD THEME TEST
1	*What did you want to do for work when you were a child? Why did you want to do that back then?*
2	*What kind of activities did you enjoy when you were a child? Do you still do those activities?*
3	*What was your number one problem when you were a child? What did you want to fix in your own life or in the world?*
4	*As a child, were you more motivated by your own thoughts and creations, by the praise of others, or by your achievements? Have your motivations changed as you grew?*
5	*What were you really good at doing as a child? When people gave you compliments, what did they say?*
6	*What was true of you as a child that is still true now?*

| 7 | What common themes do you see in your childhood? Do you see a business opportunity in those themes? |
| 8 | What was the business your parents would talk about at home? If they were in business, did you ever use your knowledge around the dinner table to impress or advance your current status? |

Consider what these questions tell you about who you are deep inside and what has always been important to you. You will probably find some truth in those memories. Also, keep in mind the kind of passport you hold. It is likely that the theme of your childhood will resemble that passport.

In this table we classified business into service and production businesses. The categories are very general in order to give you more clarity in thoughts. A restaurant would be classified to be a production-oriented business and a law firm would be a service-oriented business.

BUSINESS ORIENTATIONS			
BUSINESS MODELS	**HEART**	**HAND**	**HEAD**
SERVICE-ORIENTED BUSINESSES	I want to offer a service that benefits the greater good	I want to build a service that fixes a problem	I want to design a service that makes money
PRODUCTION-ORIENTED BUSINESS	I want to offer a product that benefits the greater good	I want to build a product that addresses needs	I want to design a product that promotes a brand

Now, do you know which country you are coming from? Once you know, you can follow the symbol in the book to find content that is most relevant to you.

Appointment with Ying @ 8am

CHAPTER 3

Packaging Everything for Sale

PACKAGING PASSION FOR SALE

"Packaging my time for sale? That is impossible to me. Only lawyers sell their time!" Hua Hua raised her voice.

Born in China, Hua Hua was in her late thirties. After starting an online selling business, she had been working with me for the past 5 years. This morning, she came in to catch me at 7am before I started my first official appointment at 8am.

There are so many times I come to work at 5am for my clients. 7am? I am ready.

Tired of Doing it for Free

Being so successful in selling goods online, Hua Hua got a lot of inquiries from relatives, friends, and friends' friends about how to start an online store. She loved to help them and realized that guiding online business ventures was something that she could do to help more people. But she was tired of doing it for free.

"With product, it is easy to put on the resale price, but with my talking to friends, what am I selling? How do I call it? Charge for chatting with me?" she chuckled.

In response to her question, I said, "Well, you are not a lawyer, but consider selling your passion. If you want to help folks to start an online store, package your passion for sale."

My 8am appointment arrived, and I had to cut my time with Hua Hua short. I promised her to come up with a concept definition of the package and pricing so that she could try to sell it. For the rest of the day, I concentrated on the business at hand. But when I was free after work, I kept my promise.

That night I came up with something very simple.

HUA HUA'S NEW PACKAGES

Online Basic - $200 – A one-time estimated one-hour consultation on the basic requirements to start an online store. Reference to the process that ITO.com has followed in the first year of operation.

Online Helping Hand - $2,000 – A one-time face to face consultation plus written guidelines to implement the online store and provide vendors and contractor information so that the store can start selling online.

Online Resources Development - $6,000 per year and a minimum 3-year commitment – Developing merchant connections in China, travel assistance once a year (including introducing producers and factories in China), and continuing to grow online exposure, with results to be measured by annual sales and profit margin. Also, .2% of the net growth will be due as commission.

About a week later, Hua Hua called and told me that she had sold her first $6k package to a client who already had a vendor connection in China. That client was dissatisfied with the products he was getting and wanted to explore more possibilities. This time, instead of giving her skill and knowledge away, Hua Hua was prepared to package her passion for sale and make a profit.

PACKAGING INTANGIBLES

The way I see our world is that if you can clearly conceptualize your specific passion, then you can package that concept and sell it.

My client Hua Hua is a Head person. Her business sells real products that you can put in a box and ship to another person. Now she wants to make the most profit possible; so I am helping her see how something you cannot hold in your hand can still be a product. For her, her knowledge and her contacts in China are her new products.

She cannot put those things in a box, but she can still sell them.

SELLING A NAME

My famous example of a Head person is Donald Trump. He understands an important truth. Because he is well-known, his name becomes a product.

Donald Trump associated his name with luxury. He lined his buildings with marble and gold. He imported the best materials and made his Manhattan creations into art. For many people, completing such creations would have been enough. It would have been enough to know that your name meant luxury.

But Donald Trump took things a step further. Yes, his name meant luxury. Because he was a Head person who always went straight to playing games with money, he thought of selling his name as a luxury brand. He was calculating another way to make money.

Then he sold the right to use his name on physical things like Cadillacs and mattresses and on non-physical things like an education certificate.[14] This was all part of the Trump brand, like the hotels and casinos. He was selling something intangible but valuable by selling his name.

SELLING POSSIBILITY

There is a story of the first big real estate deal Trump closed in Manhattan. Land in Manhattan is very expensive, and so Trump went looking for cheap land he could sell later at a profit. He found some old railroad yards that the railroad company was not using. He wanted to buy them and put apartments and shops on them that would sell for a lot of money.

The railroad was in bankruptcy, and a man named Victor Palmieri was in charge of selling the railroad assets, including the land. Trump came to Palmieri early, when not many people knew this land was for sale. This was before Trump had a big name to sell. He was just out of college and had only done the housing development in Cincinnati. So he packaged another product to sell to Palmieri: possibility.

Trump believed that he could make the railroad a lot of money to help with the bankruptcy. He believed that he knew more about how land could be used than other developers and could come up with a better plan that city officials would approve than these other developers could. Trump won over the man in charge by selling him the possibility of what he could do.

Palmieri said of Trump: "We interviewed all kinds of people who were interested in them, none of whom had what seemed like the kind of drive, backing, and imagination that would be necessary. Until this young guy Trump came along. He's almost a throwback to the nineteenth century as a promoter. He's larger than life."[15]

Though the land would not come to Trump for several years, Palmieri bought into Trump's possibility package so much that he offered him another bad property to make new: the Commodore Hotel. And the Commodore Hotel success would prove to people in Manhattan that Donald Trump's possibility package was real. He would do what he said he would do.

That would make the name of Trump worth a lot of money!
PACKAGING COMPASSION

The concept of selling is not a greedy process where I take all you have and walk away. In this endless economic circle, I make money in the community, and I spend that money in the same community. So in a micro sense, the community is the one that prospers.

CONNECTION

On a larger scale, I would say that if we can create a good business here in Des Moines, Iowa, then the positive effect will spread as far as Beijing, China, where I was born.

The big web of economic impact connects us in such a massive network. The concept of selling in this beautiful country is like announcing that you can share your value with others; when others appreciate your sharing, they will pay the appreciation back by paying you money. It is not counterintuitive to monetize your passion and your love. That is the way to do things now.

Heart people tend to become uncomfortable with the idea of selling. They want to help their clients. That is why they are in business anyway, to help. They feel better about themselves and about life if they can give something away instead of selling it, especially something you cannot hold, like their name or their knowledge of how to do something.

I see that attitude a lot in the start-up community. Often, a good idea does not generate money. If it does make money, someone will think that is spiritually wrong to profit off the good deeds. Our new start-up entrepreneurs from the Country of the Heart are passionate with they want to do. But they have skipped the process of defining the product and making solid money first.

So many times I meet with passionate start-up entrepreneurs who have good hearts and who are Heart people. Even though they have not even started the business yet, they come to me to plan how to give the profit away. "I want to donate all my profit...

I want to help," they say. A lot of times, they focus on helping but they are at a loss about how to do it.

STACIE'S NONPROFIT

I first met Stacie at the Iowa Secretary of State's office. She just came out of that office where she was asking questions to the front desk lady about how to form a nonprofit organization. Of course, Stacie needed to go to the Iowa Secretary of State's office, but she also needed to apply to the IRS to get a nonprofit status. The front desk lady did not know the IRS application for recognition of exemption under the IRS Code section of 501(c)(3). She kindly suggested that Stacie go find a law firm or CPA firm to guide her, and I happened to overhear that on my way out.

Stacie walked out, and I asked, "Hi, do you want to find a firm who can do that for you?" I extended my hand to introduce myself. Relieved, Stacie followed me to my office.

Stacie had inherited a commercial property in a small town in Iowa. Years ago, this building used to be a grocery store where kids and families would hang out. On the right of this commercial building was a Dairy Queen which was still in operation after nearly 40 years.

Out of a pure desire to help, Stacie wanted to use the place to handle donated merchandise so that people could come in to pick up what they needed. She was so focused on giving things to the needy that she did not consider her own needs: the cost of maintaining the building and running the store. She forgot the rental part of the deal – the lease package.

Of course, it was amazing of her to offer the place for the poor, but she herself was living in poverty, too. She looked so tired. One side of her car was smashed as if she had bumped into a truck. She did not have money to pay my fee, not to mention to pay for the repair of the building.

STACIE'S RATIOS

So I suggested to her that she needed to sort out how to make money out of leasing the building first before she could open the non-profit organization to help the poor. Stacie basically needed to enter a triple net lease with a renter. But Stacie did not understand triple net.

To make matters simple, I told her that for every one square foot, she would ask for $10.00. Then the renter would pay for a portion of all the other property related fees. Doing $10.00 per square foot was an easy package to sell.

Stacie had a clear concept of helping the poor by giving things away. Her products were things that were donated to her. The only element that she was lacking was money. She really needed to think about the sale price of the giveaways. But she was firm about giving a price tag of zero on all things; so I focused with her on pricing the space for rent.

I made a list of the fees and expenses that she needed to charge the renters and told her that she could not open this Goodwill-like store until she had income from rentals to cover those expenses. At the end, we had a package for sale: we packaged 5,000 sq. feet of the space for rent at $10 per sq. foot, which would cover all the expenses she would have so that she could price all products at zero.

Three months later, Stacie came back and asked me to help her to come up with a package for the things in the store. Respecting the spirit of the store, I suggested that she charge $1.00 per shopping bag. The customer could use the bag for anything in the store, but the bags were $1.00 each. We encouraged customers to buy the bags and give them to the needy so that the needy could use them to get free items from the store.

A year later, Stacie changed to charging $1.00 per item, like the Dollar Store. The business was still nonprofit, but it made enough money to pay for Stacie's salary. Stacie learned through experience that she couldn't work for free. She needed to package her passion and take care of herself in order to give to others.

Fair and Kind

George Zimmer, CEO of Men's Wearhouse, says something that all Heart people in business need to hear: "Don't be afraid to charge enough for your products or services."[16] This is true! You cannot let fear or concern stop you from being fair to yourself.

After all, not charging what you are owed is being unkind to yourself and your business. If you have employees, then not charging enough is being unkind to those employees. How can you be fair to them if you don't have any money?

Also, aren't you worth as much as an employee?

Think of the businesses you enjoy, the place where you buy coffee or get your haircut. You want to show your appreciation of other businesses with your money. In the same way, let other people appreciate you. Give them the same chance they give you.

Conscious Work

In a talk with Sir Ken Robinson, Eckhart Tolle talks about finding consciousness and peace in your work. Tolle uses the example of a person working in a restaurant who does not enjoy his job. The people who eat at the restaurant and the other workers there can all feel the negative energy, and they stay away from this person.

Tolle says that maybe the answer for this person is not to find a different job but to bring a different attention to the same job. Really taking care to place plates gently and to serve people well will create a different energy that customers and coworkers can all sense.

And maybe, Tolle says, someone at that restaurant will become friendly and curious about that person. Maybe the curious person will have a new opportunity to offer the conscious worker. That opportunity only comes when the energy is good. And the good energy comes not from doing a different thing but from doing something in a different way: not *what*, but *how*.[17]

So for you, if you don't like the idea of making money from your work, what needs to change is not the way business works but the way you think about it. Think of it as a positive exchange that goes both ways. Think of yourself as being just as valuable as your customer and your work as being just as valuable as their money. You are participating in a positive exchange where both people are equal.

Everybody can feel good about that kind of sale!

PACKAGING PRODUCTS

Some people who come to my office already know this truth. They are ready to package a product for sale; they just want advice about how to begin. A lot of these people are Hand people. They love what they do, and they see value in their work.

THE BLACK BOX

My client Denise came to my office with a black box in her hand containing a product she invented. She knew that her product had value. She wanted to commercialize the product.

The box had an opening to receive kitchen waste; on the bottom that waste would be released into a water hose. The kitchen waste in the box would turn into liquid and could come out mixed with the water to water growing plants. The box could be big or small. It could also be made to any shape the customer liked so it would fit the landscape. This invention had the potential to turn a backyard into an organic farm. What a concept!

The challenge was to price the product by imagining what the customer would want it to be. There would be alternatives in size, in shape, and in delivery. So Denise and I spent a lot of spreadsheet time together to build a cost list by size and by molding of a fixed list of shapes. That way, we could cut uncertainty for consumers so that we wouldn't lose potential buyers.

Some great advice I have heard is: "When developing a product, make sure that it is market driven. Great products that lack champions, identified markets, or customers are destined for failure."[18] Denise and I considered all of those factors and came up with a very simple way of pricing the product.

Instead of letting consumers determine the product, we introduced the product by measuring how much of the ground they need to cover. For instance, if the coverage is only a 10 by 10 flower bed, then the black box would sell for $49.00 on the original shape. Out of a million possibilities, we focused on only three established styles – The Rock shape; The Stool, and the Watering Can. Each of these shapes would add additional dollars to the base price. The package was easy to understand and fun to see, and the sales instantly picked up.

Today, her products are sold worldwide not only in homes but also on farms.

With time, Denise learned that the Rock was the best seller. So she went on and made more products under the Rock. Now there are Moon Rock, Mars Rock, and so on.

Double Time

Another great way to package your specialty for sale is to come up with an unusual combination of services. I have another client who does just that. Tom is a devoted personal trainer. Normally, a personal trainer trains by the hour and bills for his time.

Tom wanted to be different, and he saw a unique opportunity in the fact that he speaks Spanish. So he began taking clients for personal training and teaching them Spanish at the same time. His theory was that when your body is actively moving, your memory is working at its best. At the same time, you could exercise and also acquire a new language. So Tom's clients stayed with him, even though they were paying double the fees.

SPACE AND ENERGY

You can be like Tom and offer a service or a combination of services as your product. This is how Elon Musk started. Internet apps and businesses are services that you pay to get. When Elon Musk created Zip2 and PayPal, he was creating services that people could buy. They were buying his knowledge of how to get around a city or how to transfer money to someone instantly without a bank.

Elon Musk next moved to another service and a product.

The other service was space travel. Musk's company Space X would provide the service of transportation to the International Space Station and to earth orbit, and later they would provide the service of transportation to Mars. These were services that only governments had provided until Musk decided to provide them.[19]

But Musk asked, "Why not? Why can't I provide this service?" He saw opportunity in that question, and he knew that he could make something to profit from that opportunity.

The product that Musk decided to offer was the Tesla car. He had wanted to create an electric car for a long time. When he heard about the hard work and creativity of Martin Eberhard and Marc Tarpenning on the Tesla car, Musk invested $6.5 million and became chairman of the company. He knew that these engineers could help him bring his dream of creating a practical electric car to life.[20]

In the businesses that Musk chose to pursue, he knew what his end product would be. He always had a very clear vision of what he was packaging to sell to the consumer. He knew that at the end of all his work, he would be able to sell a new car, a ride to space, a bank transaction, or a route to the best pizza in town.

One thing that makes Elon Musk such a success is that he knows what products people are going to want before they know they want them. He knows this because he knows what he wants and follows his instincts.

This could be a good idea for you, too. What do you want? How can you package that to sell?

HIDDEN PRODUCTS

I will tell you a little secret. Tax and accounting services are not all that I sell at Community CPA. I know that people come to me for more than help with money.

They come to me for acceptance and friendliness. They come to me for patient communication. They come to me for understanding and reassurance.

Yes, those qualities are my passion! And I package them to sell along with my financial services. If you are my client, you get my passion along with my talent.

ENJOY THE ACCENT

Here is a good example. I have an ear for accents; so I enjoy listening to all kinds of them.

While I was growing up in the melting pot of Toronto, Canada, I learned an easy way to make friends. When I met someone, I liked to guess where they were from based on the accent I heard. I would say, "Oh, are you from Australia?"

Many times, my new acquaintance would be thrilled and say: "Wow! You are the only person who guessed I am Australian! People think I am British all the time!"

Such compliments from my new friends and new clients make me beam with excitement when I see someone new to the USA. Out of habit, I pay attention to how people speak English. At the right time, I surprise them by saying, "You are from Canada!" These easy discoveries help me to bring new clients to my business and to build a new friendship with someone I've just met.

Even if you don't enjoy the many accents as I do, you should be accepting of them. In today's business world, it is almost a required skill to be able to connect with business affiliates who speak English with strong accents. If you find yourself uneasy around thick accents, or if you struggle to make sense of what a new acquaintance is saying, take a deep breath and be honest. "Excuse me, I love your accent, but can you please speak a little slower so that I can understand what you are saying?"

Immigrants often take things very seriously because their lack of experience makes everything feel so intense in their new environment. This could be their first job in the USA, and they just do not think that they can be understood easily because of their accent. Nervousness might even make it harder to speak! Acceptance and encouragement from others would help the immigrant improve his English.

Don't Nod Your Head

If you are an immigrant and English is not your first language, the worst mistake in communication is automatically nodding your head as if you understood what was said. Pretending does no one any good. And both professionals and immigrants do it.

My client Peter did not know much English when he arrived. He told me that he knew how to say three words: Yes, No, and Okay. When someone would come up to him and ask him a question, he would say Yes. If he got a funny look, he would try No and Okay!

But Peter has learned good English in the USA. English is one of six languages that he knows. That is one smart guy!

They Are Smart!

We need to give immigrants to the USA time to get comfortable. Also, we need to overcome our own mental barriers by simply recognizing that an accent is part of a culture, not a bad habit or a mark of low intelligence. Accent has nothing to do with how smart immigrants are. It is just a mark of someone who's new to the USA.

If you enjoy being open-minded or want to be at home with folks who are new to the USA, start with appreciating and listening to their unique accents. I do not speak Spanish, but I have many Spanish-speaking clients who speak strongly accented English. These folks often tell me that I understand them perfectly. After hearing their accents for so long, I do understand them.

And I enjoy the sound of their speaking. Their accent helps connect me to these hardworking people. I look at the people and think, "They speak a language that I do not, and they are smart for that!"

Packaging Acceptance

So enjoy the sound of their accents, and see the world through the eyes of these immigrants. Don't let someone's accent become a barrier between you and them. Use it instead to bring you together.

Like me, you can package acceptance and non-judgmental approaches for connecting with people and making them feel at home. Your best qualities are part of your service. No matter what passport you hold and how you started your business, I think you should include this package in your price tag. That would increase your value without causing cash outflow; it only requires you to have compassion and be non-judgmental.

It is clear that packaging something to sell does not require you to have an earth-shattering discovery. You could charge for your knowledge like Hua Hua or charge for your space, like Stacie. You might have an invention like Denise or a unique skill combination, like Tom. But there is something more important to be included in your package to sell – sell that without shame and hesitation – that is compassion and acceptance.

REFLECTION #5: PRICING FOR "THE FREE PACKAGE"

Find one thing right now you are doing for free, and imagine how you could sell it for a price. Think of Donald Trump selling his name. A name is normally for free so we can be called freely by others. But in business, the "Trump" brand has value.

Then remember Hua Hua's free service to folks who wants to do online selling.

	YOUR "FREE" PACKAGE
1	*List all the ways this free thing that you do for people has real value. That is your identified market research.*
2	*Think of the people who come to you to get it for free. They are your customer base.*
3	*Try to package this free thing as if you were going to put in on a shelf or a website to sell. This is how you will get champions (or super fans) who will love your product and give you word-of-mouth advertising.*

Below is a guide to keep in mind for conducting research and determining your customer and super fan base.

MARKET RESEARCH CATEGORIES			
CATEGORY	**HEART**	**HAND**	**HEAD**
IDENTIFIED MARKET RESEARCH	*Servie-driven*	*Product-driven*	*Idea-driven*
CUSTOMER BASE	*Service-driven*	*Product-driven*	*Idea-driven*
SUPER FANS	*Service-driven*	*Product-driven*	*Idea-driven*

REFLECTION #6: MAKING YOUR BUSINESS UNIQUE

Remember how I identified some of my good qualities and packaged them for sale? As for Community CPA, people know that they are coming for quality and reliable financial care; also for empathy, friendliness, and easy communication. For someone who does not speak a ton of English, with our firm speaking 9 different languages, folks are comfortable to come in.

	YOUR UNIQUE BUSINESS
1	*Think of your best qualities. What makes you an enjoyable person or a good friend?*
2	*How do these qualities relate to your business? Remember Eckhart Tolle. You may be doing the same **what** as everyone else, but you can do it with a different **how.***
3	*What unique combination comes from your business plus your qualities? I am a compassionate, friendly accountant. Are you a patient listener who arranges flowers? Are you a high-energy, positive engineer?*

Use the guide that follows to practice writing up a description of the kind of business owner you are and the kind of product you provide. For example:

MARKET RESEARCH CATEGORIES			
ELEMENTS	HEART	HAND	HEAD
Basic Product/ Service	CPA Service	Pho noodles	A new home to sell
ADD UNIQUENESS	*We open on Saturday. When all the professional firms are closed, we stay open.*	*Normally, the noodle comes out steaming hot. We make a check mark for what temperature clients like.*	*Advertise that the building is designed with Feng Shui in mind and a guaranteed blessing.*
SUPER FANS	*Service-driven*	*Product-driven*	*Idea-driven*

CHAPTER 4

Choose a Tax Structure

YOUR VISA TO THE LAND OF BUSINESS

Because I am an immigrant, I relate a lot of my understanding of entering the Land of Business to the immigration process for coming to the USA. Starting a business is no different from migrating from your home country to the USA. Choosing a business entity to operate your start up business is almost like choosing a type of visa to enter the new world – we call it the Land of Business.

For me, I entered the USA with a TN visa and then later changed it to an H1 before I eventually received my immigrant visa (green card). Some people simply visit the USA as a tourist; so a B2 visitor's visa would work. For others, there are L1, O1, and several other visa types. These are simply ways to get you over to the USA so you can start enjoying, living, or working in the USA.

Selecting a tax entity at the time of starting your business is like getting a visa so you can enter the Land of Business and start working on your business. Without this selection process, you can get into real trouble.

THE IRS AND THE IES

Many hardworking, good-citizen immigrant entrepreneurs run into trouble when they do not know the rules. To help immigrants learn the basics of business, I started a series of conferences which is called the Immigrant Entrepreneurs Summit. These IES conferences are business equalizers. They give out business secrets to immigrants and to business immigrants. They teach in many different ways about tax structure selections.

Interestingly some immigrant folks told me that IES looks like the IRS, Jr., because the difference in the names is only one letter. In fact, the idea for IES came from a pile of IRS notices that landed on my desk back in 2007. If a proper visa was selected and used, the story would have been nonexistent.

The IRS Letters

At that time, Community CPA was located next to the Fish Market. One day, Lem - an Asian lady who had just finished shopping next door - came in carrying all of her groceries and asked to see me. She pulled out of her pocket a stack of letters from the IRS and handed them to me.

Pointing at her grocery bags and opening one of them to show me what was in it, she said, "This is all for my business." She was telling me that she purchased things from next door, and they were all for her business use. So the bags in her hands were not personal purchases.

Based on what she had just said and a quick review of some of the letters, I figured she had a retail grocery business that had been operating for at least three years. I also noticed that she had a limited liability company (LLC) set up for that business. The IRS letters suggested that she had not filed tax returns for her LLC entity. They were assessing more than $50,000 in tax, interest, and penalties.

In other words, Lem entered the Land of Business with one type of visa, but she had not done anything to be in compliance with the visa.

MY IRS IS LITTLE

After about an hour or so, following a lot of waiting and finally speaking with an IRS agent, I had a solution for her. She needed to dissolve the tax structure that had been formed but had never been used, and she needed to amend three years' worth of federal and state income tax returns. On top of that, I would file her sales taxes for the past 3 years.

"Really? I did what? Structure for what? LLC? " She was in disbelief.

Like Lem, any immigrant-owned small businesses that started the business without any understanding of their tax structure may be doing taxes all wrong. Things like an income statement, balance sheet, and tax compliance are sometimes unknown to them. How can they comply with regulations and rules if they don't understand, or even worse, if they had never heard of them?

So I explained everything, slowly and with great detail, to Lem. At the end, she gave me a big hug and said, "Ying, where can I go to learn this? My IRS is little."

I chuckled, because I knew what she meant was that her IRS knowledge was limited. I replied: "The IRS is not little!"

IES IS BORN

The following year, I met with two other community business leaders in town, and the three of us started this nonprofit called Immigrant Entrepreneurs Summit – a place and time where practical business knowledge could be shared without a price tag.

The IRS is not and will never be little. The goal of IES is to educate and help entrepreneurs, like Lem, Peter, Jose, and many more. IES can make tax and accounting compliance simpler and more streamlined.

The IES mantra is, "Let's grow together." More than two hundred business owners, representing more than 30 countries, attended the first IES in 2008. IES attendees have been growing by leaps and bounds since then. Nine hundred came to the 2017 event. Each year, more and more immigrant businessmen and women leave the "my IRS is little" stage to become seasoned businessmen and businesswomen who go on to accomplish great things.

IES educates folks about federal and state regulatory compliance as well as industry-specific requirements. After all, being a great citizen of the Land of Business does require all business immigrants to know the rules. They all know how to use their financial binoculars!

My friend who said IRS is little made a mistake because she did not understand tax structures. She did not realize that she was literally going through immigration the second time. As this time she was going from the Country of the Hand to the Land of Business, she needed a proper visa to conduct her business.

COMMON TAX STRUCTURES

Lem started her business in a tax structure called LLC. She did not know to file a return for it; so she got a notice from the IRS claiming that she had unpaid tax due.

Often I have my clients ask me: "What is the tax structure my business should have?"

My answer is always a bit longer than they expect. Because sometimes I even have to ask: "Are you happily married?"

Selecting structure is an art of business life.

There are four ordinary and popular business tax structures, or you may say business entities, that you can situate your business in when you are starting up. Each one is like a different kind of visa for entering the Land of Business. There are Sole Proprietorship, LLC Partnership, S corp, and C corp.

SOLE PROPRIETOR

For the longest time in US business history, sole proprietorship has been the way to go. You need no special legal service or setup to begin your business – I mean you may enter the Land of Business with no visa. You are simply just entitled to have a business. You use your name and your social security number as your business ID. You are your business.

THE COMMUNIST VISA

Yes, as far as the government is concerned, *you* are the business. At the end of the calendar year, you file Schedule C under 1040 to report your business activities. Then you are all set.

Schedule C brings your business and your personal finance into one. Keep in mind that the C in Schedule C represents the communist way of doing business because you and your business are sharing the wealth and risk together. You and your business are one.

When your business is at a loss, you are allowed to use your salary income or other income to offset the business loss. As the result of that, you could get some refund back if you have income to offset the loss. In some extreme cases, you can lose so much money on this sole proprietor business that you would not pay taxes for a number of years till you offset all your losses with your income within the next 20 years.

If you made money under a Schedule C Sole Proprietor business, your income would be treated just like your W2 income that is subject to both income tax and self-employment tax.

LIMITS OF SOLE PROPRIETORSHIP

Many of my clients who were born in the USA and grew up in the USA would naturally know this way of doing business. But for the immigrants who come to the USA, they may or may not be qualified to be a Sole Proprietorship business, depending on their visa type. As they might not have a work permit, they cannot work as a sole proprietor.

For instance, my client Sandra came to the USA on an H4 visa. Her husband works as a professor in the university on an H1 visa, and her visa type would not allow her to be a sole proprietor. Starting a business for her properly means she must look for a different tax structure which will not violate her visa restrictions.

My client Tom uses this tax structure. He has been doing personal training plus Spanish lessons for a couple of years by now. He works as a police sergeant for the city full time.

In 2017 when we met, he used Schedule C to report his income and expenses. That year we decided that Tom remain as Schedule C because his side business has no conflicts of interest with his position as a police officer. Plus he has not made more than $25,000 net profit in a year to be economically sound to move to a different tax structure. You see, tax structure is something you can change.

As a personal trainer, Tom did not have a lot of expenses other than the classes and training that he has to take himself as part of the qualification to be a personal trainer. I met Tom again at the end of 2018 for tax planning. He provided me with his profit projection for 2018.

He would net $58,000 profit. So I calculated that he would end up paying $8,700 to self-employment tax and another 30% (which is $17,400) to income tax. He would need to pay $26,100 tax out of the $58,000 net profit he made.

Tom made a funny face at me when I told him this. He said: "Can I get a different visa?"

THE LLC DILEMMA

No! LLC is not the answer for Tom, as a single member LLC is defaulted back to sole proprietorship for tax filing purposes.

Forming a Limited Liability Company seems to be very popular among new businesses. If you ask an attorney about getting started with a business, a lot of the time an LLC will be the recommendation. John is an attorney friend of mine. He tells me that an LLC is easy to form, and it is easier to maintain.

I agree that an LLC is one of the most flexible entity structures you can deploy if you can understand all the flexible joints. The main joints are the following: membership units, net profit, operating loss, and member equity.

An LLC may have more than one member. The tax treatment is different between a single member LLC and a multi-member LLC. The tax liability is also different for each member, depending on what his or her position is in the LLC. (Here I am assuming the default rule for LLC tax filing. Later I will talk about LLC's election to be taxed differently from the default rule.)

LLC members can decide on how to share profit and how to share loss. The sharing of profit and loss do not need to be same as the equity split. For instance, a two-member LLC can have equal ownership, which also means the equity split is equal. However, if one member is working on the business full time, to be fair, that member could share 80% of profit, and the other member would only get 20% profit. Equity does not determine how each member would share the profit or loss. Keep that in mind.

THE ERROR MESSAGE

My client Jose had already started his equipment repair business in 2004 as an LLC when I first met him. He came to me because he could not properly file his LLC tax filing. His issue was typical.

Jose has no paper. He has no work permit. But he has an ITIN

(Individual Tax Identification Number).

He went to an attorney and formed an LLC by registering with the Secretary of State. The attorney did not ask him about his status, and Jose had no reason to tell the attorney; so a single-member LLC was registered with the state.

When the time came to report tax, first was the sales tax reporting. Jose realized that he needed to have an ID (I mean a tax ID number) to register for sales tax with the state; so he tried with his ITIN, but that didn't work.

At the year-end LLC tax filing time, Jose tried to file Schedule C under his 1040 because he was a single member LLC. Then the problem showed up again. Recall that Jose did not have a work permit; so by USCIS visa regulations, he would not be able to work as a sole proprietor.

His tax preparer told him that his ID was no good with their tax software. It caused the system to flash an error message saying, "Invalid ID for self-employment tax calculation."

Jose came to my office wondering if I had a system that would not give out the warning like the other tax firm's system did.

Knowing Jose's immigration status, I asked Jose about why he set up an LLC, and he said: "I went to the attorney, and he told me to set up an LLC. He did not ask me any other questions. I brought my ITIN with me, but he did not ask for it."

It is understandable that not everyone can imagine every businessperson's situation correctly. If the law office does not deal with immigrants on a regular basis, the attorney will not be able to advise about the situation correctly.

A single-member LLC is equivalent to a sole proprietorship for tax filing. It is understandable that if you do not have a valid work authorization, you cannot work legally in the USA as a sole proprietor.

The problem for an ITIN holder goes further; for instance, he does not qualify for Social Security and Medicare benefits. Therefore, there is no accumulation of Social Security and Medicare benefit for the ITIN worker. Anyone who earns Social Security and Medicare benefits must be authorized to work in the USA. That's a harsh reality, but it is the plain truth.

Multi-Member LLC

An LLC with multiple members works differently than a single-member LLC. Multiple members simply mean that each member can have different roles. In this setting, a person without a work permit or a social security number can be a partner. The distribution would not be subject to self-employment tax as long as the income the partner is getting is not payment for his or her labor. It can simply be a return on investment and profit sharing.

If Jose is in a multi-member partnership LLC, he would have filed 1065 instead of 1040 Schedule C. A partnership filing uses a form called 1065. The filing of a partnership return would drive the bottom line – profit or loss - all to the partners' personal return through a form called K1. So in reality, partnership is in the same vein as the sole proprietorship. The difference is that the K1 would be filed in Schedule E, not Schedule C.

A work authorization is still required to receive the income as an active participant in the business, and self-employment tax is still calculated for the member. The only exception is that if a member is a passive investor, that member's income will not be subject to self-employment tax.

In other words, if an ITIN holder is a partner in the partnership, the correct way of handling the payout to this ITIN holder is to pay the partner as a passive investor and get a K1 that does not subject that partner to self-employment tax.

Another client called Sergei has no paper. He was born in the USA but has no paper. Don't ask me why, because I can get really sad for folks to be trapped in such a situation that automatic citizenship by birth on US soil did not hold. Sergei and his brother Pyotr are well-known local home flippers. They are 50% and 50%

on profit, but if there is a loss one year, the partnership will divide loss 20% to Sergei and 80% to Pyotr, because Pyotr has other income to offset his loss.

S CORP FOR SOCIALISM

An S corp is another type of tax entity one can use to organize a business. In terms of being a shareholder of an S corp, the million dollar question is, "Who can be the shareholder of an S corp?" Although anyone who meets the IRS resident tests can be a S corp shareholder, there are various issues in practice if the shareholder is an ITIN person. It's best we just think only U.S. citizens, permanent residents, or single-member LLCs owned by a US citizen or a permanent resident can be owners of an S corp. Furthermore, the IRS limits S corps to have no more than 100 shareholders.

Nowadays, many businesses are making themselves S Corps. There are several considerations for this type of structure.

A Tax Escape

S corp profit distribution does not get imposed self-employment tax.

For instance, if you made $100,000 net profit under a sole proprietorship or under a single-member LLC or by being an active member of a multi-member LLC, you would have paid income tax plus self-employment tax. Self-employment tax is about 15% in addition to the income tax you would pay at the year-end tax filing time.

Assume your income tax rate is 20%. Add the 15% self-employment tax, and you would pay total of 35% tax on the $100,000 profit we talked about. Your total federal tax due would be $35,000. In this case, we are not calculating state taxes, and just on the federal tax return, your cash payment out would be $35,000.

However, for an S corp, this $100,000 is not subject to self-employment tax at all. Only income tax is applicable. As the income tax rate is 20%, the total cash outlay for tax is $20,000.

S Corps and Losses

Sometimes an S corp is the best choice for handling a loss. Emily's restaurant was set up as an S Corporation. She is a US citizen, and she put forward a large amount of money to get the restaurant going. These equipment purchases can be written off right away if we utilize some tax incentives.

Anticipating the first couple of years having a loss or making moderate profit, we set up an S corp for her. Her husband makes a stable, high, salaried income. So on the first-year return, we had a $150,000 loss to offset her husband's $250,000 W-2 income. Emily received a $35,500 refund from her joint return at the end of the year.

The Socialist Visa

The S corp Wikipedia says: "An S corporation, for United States federal income tax purposes, is a closely held corporation that makes a valid election to be taxed under Subchapter S of Chapter 1 of the Internal Revenue Code."[21]

While English is my second language, to help my client remember the characteristic of an S corp, I call it a socialism corporation. The spirit of socialism is about being fair and equal to all members of society. Applying that spirit to a corporation, S corp means to be fair and equal to all shareholders and employees.

The spirit of leveling the playing field calls for company benefits to be spread among shareholders and employees, otherwise the shareholder cannot deduct that expense under the company expenses. The shareholder special perks need to be treated as income to the shareholder and be taxed on the shareholder's personal return.

S corp is a corporation where shareholder benefits can only be deducted as company expenses when they are peanut buttered to all eligible employees. As the Three Musketeers say, "One for all, and all for one!" The Musketeers would have done great with an S corp.

Emily was not into company benefits at all when she just started her S corp. The first-year big loss was followed by two more years of losses. Once she closed the restaurant and continued on chef training and placement agency work, she started to have profit.

She emailed me: "Ying, when you do tax planning for me this year, could you let me know what kind of benefit I can give to myself and also deduct it out from my business?"

I knew she wanted me to reply: "All of it!"

That was not the case; so I replied: "Emily, do you recall what S stands for in your tax structure? S for socialism. Unless the benefit is going to be given to your other two employees, you will not be able to deduct any as company expenses. Owner/employees holding 2% or more of the company's shares cannot receive tax-free benefits."

Because of the way Emily wants to do business and handle company benefits, maybe she will change to a C corp when her profits rise.

C CORP FOR CAPITALISTS

A C corporation, on the contrary, does not need to spread the benefit to all employees, yet the company can still deduct the benefit before paying taxes. C in this case stands for capitalist. It is a corporation that is capable of benefiting and protecting a few.

Remember I mentioned to you that when clients ask me which tax structure they should be using for their new business, I sometimes have a need to know if they are happily married. It wasn't a joke, and I got negative answers not only once or twice but many times.

Say you want to start a business in the midst of your ugly divorce. I would recommend you set up C corp so at least you would not bring the business into the divorce proceedings.

Corporate Perks

A C corp is taxed differently from the above entities. It has its own tax rate, and it does not merge the final profit or loss with the owner's personal tax return. I always tell my folks, "Just imagine that the C corp is a grown-up child of yours. You cannot report that adult child as your dependent anymore. The child is out of your tax return and has his or her own. If your child messed up, as he is your adult child, you are not responsible for his deed and debt."

Since C is for capitalism, it is generally used to protect the interest of capitalists. As the executive or shareholder of the company, you can develop special compensation and benefits inside the corporation. It is a vehicle to benefit a few. Benefit that can still be legally and properly deducted does not need to be made available to all employees.

The shareholder can drive a company car for business-related activities, and the expenses related to the usage and maintenance of the car are fully deductible as company expenses. Just remember to keep records. The shareholder can have a better retirement package than regular employees at the company. If the company buys a house for use by a company executive (also a shareholder) but not for every employee, it is still possible to be deducted as company expenses. That's what a C corp is.

A Solution for Jose

A C corp comes into play for many other reasons. In Jose's case, he should have formed a C corp to begin with. Because Jose does not have a work permit, his C corp cannot hire him as an employee. However, anyone can be the shareholder of C corp, black or white, visa or no visa, citizen or foreigner, and so on. Jose had an LLC, but if he had a C corp instead, he would have had no issue with filing his first-year company tax.

Even though Jose does not have a work permit, he is eligible to receive dividend income on a regular basis from his company, as we have changed his LLC to be a C corp. The word "change" means we have elected Jose's LLC to be treated as C corp for tax purposes. The election may be done late as long as you seek late filing relief.

Jose legally, properly receives dividend income from his company. Remember he wanted to do everything right when we just met? Of course, Jose is paying more taxes than folks who can get W2 income, but Jose is literally happy to pay more taxes as long as his income is legitimate.

Jose takes the dividend to his personal tax return and simply files a regular 1040 with the dividend income.

Recall that when he formed the LLC, he did not get an employer tax identification number. When we filed the election for him, we also applied for an EIN number for him. He uses the EIN number to pay employee payroll taxes, sales tax, and income tax and to issue his dividend to himself.

Now that the EIN number is here, Jose never needs to use his ITIN number to conduct his business.

He is all business.

MUSK'S NARROW ESCAPE

Elon Musk had made hundreds of millions from his investment in PayPal. But Musk was more interested in his products than in money. So he invested that money into Solar City, which his cousins had started, and into SpaceX and Tesla, his own companies.

At first, Musk's investments went well. People were excited about his new products. Many wanted to invest in his companies. Some customers who had only seen a prototype of a Tesla at a distance or who had only heard about it from others were begging Musk to take $100,000 from them to prepay for a Tesla.

But then Musk ran into complications at SpaceX and at Tesla. At SpaceX, that his engineers encountered problems was understandable because they were building the rockets from scratch. They were reinventing what NASA had done in the 1960s and trying to do it with far fewer people for much less money. Still, each Falcon rocket that exploded caused huge disappointment and ate up more of Musk's money.

As far as Tesla was concerned, the company experienced two kinds of problems. One was a problem with the way the company was being run. They were sourcing parts of the car from all over the world and having the cars assembled in different stages at different places. Part of the car was put together in France; another part was put together in England. The car was finished in the USA. That was expensive.

Another problem was with the technology of the car. The car had to be both safe and light. The car had to be both efficient and functional. Sometimes the engineers wanted changes that Musk thought were ugly, and sometimes Musk wanted changes that the engineers thought were unnecessary. They had to compromise.

But the compromises meant delay. Soon all of those people who had begged Musk to take their money for a Tesla were wondering, "Where is my car?" And investors were wondering, "When are you going to start selling cars and making me money?"

In 2008, the banks in the USA were in trouble. They had gambled on the housing market in foolish ways and lost money. The whole economy suffered. People were panicking. And as public companies, SpaceX and Tesla suffered when people panicked.

There was another problem, too. Elon Musk had run out of money. All those hundreds of millions of dollars from PayPal were gone.

"I could either pick SpaceX or Tesla or split the money I had left between them. That was a rough decision. If I split the money, maybe both of them would die. If I gave the money to just one company, the probability of it surviving was greater, but then it would mean certain death for the other company. I debated that over and over."[22]

But Musk didn't want to choose. He gave Tesla a loan from SpaceX, and then he started having to ask people for money to keep his companies going. Some of the employees at Tesla gave him their savings for an investment.

Because of the way Tesla was structured, Musk's investors owed him support in exchange for the hope of profit. Now that he was in trouble, he turned to his investors to raise money. Most of them promised more, but one company held out. This was VantagePoint, and Musk was sure that they wanted to fire him and take control of Tesla. Then they could sell the company or its technology to another car maker and get some money. VantagePoint refused to help Tesla.

So Musk bluffed the investors. He said that he would come up with all of the money by himself. That would cut them out of some future profits and leave Musk with a bigger share of the company. Musk could not afford to do this, but he pretended he could so that he could save his company.

Besides, saying he will do something himself is just the way someone from the Country of the Hand will deal with a problem. Something I have noticed about a Hand person is independence. If you are a Hand person and you are from the Country of the

Hand, you want to do all of the jobs in your company to make sure that they get done right.

Three things happened to save Musk. A company founded by some of his cousins, Everdream, sold to Dell and got him about $15 million. Then, on December 23, 2008, NASA gave SpaceX $1.6 billion to make twelve launches to the ISS. And the very next day, the Tesla investors relented and gave Musk the money to keep Tesla going.

The Tesla deal happened hours before Musk was going to have to confess that he could not make payroll. In a few hours, he would have lost everything.[23]

In this story "lost everything" mean everything that was invested in the company. It means all the investors would lose, too. If Musk had some millions saved in his personal account, it would not be lost at all.

This story about Elon Musk teaches me that business is full of encountering risks. Like Musk, his companies, not him personally, are facing the risks. If he organized his business under Sole Proprietor, his story would be very different.

WHICH VISA DO YOU NEED?

Not all visas are right for all immigrants to the USA. In the same way, not all tax structures are right for all businesses. Natural-born Americans tend to pick Sole Proprietorship or LLC; lawyers tend to organize young companies under an LLC. These structures may or may not be right for you.

HOUSING AND BUSINESS DEVELOPMENT

A tax structure is like a house which protects you from rain or snow. You select a house to fit your family. If you are single, obviously a small condo or a one-room house would be enough for you. And if you have 7 kids in the family, of course you can have a bigger home.

So for your business, it is the same thing. You're going to choose the house for your particular business. You may say, "Well, why is this tax structure important? Why can't I do my business now and decide it later?"

Yes, of course you can do that, but it is not the best practice.

Every tax structure has a different way of paying taxes. That's why you want to select the right one. It is like moving; You want to get into a house right away that you can afford but that also has enough room for your family to grow.

This talk of finding a structure to fit you reminds me of the way Eckhart Tolle says that you approach life as a conscious person. A conscious person changes his or her way of living depending on the situation. Eckhart talked about three ways: acceptance, enjoyment, and enthusiasm.

In the business world, you would approach selection of the tax structures in similar ways – you make a conscious choice depending on the situation. You may change your mind and select a different kind of structure. That is okay, and it is allowed by the tax code. That action to select different tax structure is election. Your choice of tax structures should lead you to enjoyment of tax efficiency and give you excitement for the work ahead.

You noticed that I did not say "enjoyment of tax reduction."

Eckhart said: If you are doing something you do not naturally like but something you have to do, you bring acceptance to that thing you are doing. If paying taxes are making you sick to your stomach and you gather hatred around the tax bills, then it is time to change your thinking. In general, the more money you make, the more taxes you will pay. Paying more taxes this year than last year is a symbol that you-are-doing-better-than-last-year. As long as your tax structure is current and your books and records are managed accurately, be grateful. You ended up paying more tax? Isn't it a point of celebration?

I know very few people who would say that they are enthusiastic about cleaning toilets or paying taxes. But you know what? There are clients of mine who would be so grateful about paying tax to the IRS. Lem was one of them. She was the lady who brought a bag of IRS notices and told me that the IRS is little. She had so much trouble with the IRS because her tax structure was messed up. We resolved the issue for her, and she even received some refund back from both federal and state. She was happy, and I was proud.

Years later, Lem's business is still in operation. Each quarter, she comes by to pay her quarterly estimate taxes. Yesterday I saw her, and she said to me: "I paid $200 more to my estimated tax this year; I am doing so good I should pay in more."

I am enthusiastic about paying taxes! I have a brother who is afflicted with cerebral palsy. When I lived in Canada, there folks complained about taxes, but I would never. Seeing how much the government was helping my own brother, I was happy paying my fair share to the government so they could continue to help folks like my brother.

Yes, I do pay my fair share. But I do not pay tips to the IRS.

For you, don't set your goal on paying as little tax as possible. There is another goal that is worth setting. Set a goal to explore ways to pay tax more efficiently. Nothing is wrong with paying tax, but you just do not need to pay tips.

Maybe choosing a tax structure can be a chance to exist in a conscious way. You can accept that you are doing something necessary for the health and strength of your business. You can enjoy thinking of the possibilities that a new tax structure will give you. It may save you problems or create new ways of doing things. You can see how shaping your business in a new way supports your life goals or adds to the total happiness of other people.

ELECTION TIME

When folks begin a business and the business has losses, if the business owner is a US citizen and permanent resident, an S corp would be the first choice, followed by an LLC.

The LLC requires the business owner who is actively working in the business to pay self-employment tax. So when the company is losing money, the owner can deduct it as an ordinary loss without subjecting it to passive loss restriction. Basically, you can offset your loss with your other income on the same return.

If the business is making money, being an S corp would save the owner from paying self-employment tax on the entire profit. Emily started as an S corp to help with the early stage losses.

We saw that a C corp, not an LLC, was the best fit for Jose. It was really what he should have done at the beginning. But he had already worked in the company as a single member LLC; so now what could he do?

He elected his LLC to be a C corp. Yes, that could be done, and election could be retroactively applied to the beginning of the year. Now with the election, he no longer had the issue with self-employment tax calculation. He filed 1120 for his C corp, and he filed 1099-Div income for his 1040.

Others have benefitted from the same strategy. Hua Hua, who is successful in everything she does, structured her online business as an S corporation. That business was taking off and profit was over $450,000 within a short period of time. With this $450,000 K1 income from her S corp and salary of $100,000 from her company, she was paying the top rate of income tax rate on her 1040.

Recall that we started her online consultation service on top of this online business. Anticipating more income to come in, we set up this new business as a C corp. The reason for the tax structure was not the same as Jose's reason. In Hua Hua's case, we were aiming to lower the tax rate from 39.5% to 21%, because the C corp has a flat rate of 21%.

Hua Hua was more than happy to pay the 21% under the C

corp. She said to me: "If I need to pay, I need to pay; I want to do it right and pay what I need to pay."

I sometimes say to myself that those immigrants are the real supporters of the country's economy.

The scenarios of best use of tax structures are endless. Just know that entity switching is possible. Just like in Jose's case, we simply elected the LLC to be treated as C corp. You can always change your entity type if it does not fit.

There is a five-year stay rule in place which sometimes prevents you from changing entity type too often. But if you really need to change, explore the exception to the rules. If worst comes to worst, you can you can go ahead, do a brand-new structure, and adopt a Doing Business As name to be the same as the company you just closed. In this case, your customers are still seeing you as the old company, and you can still deposit your customer's check – which was written to your DBA name - to your newly established business bank account.

Election is a useful strategy.

REFLECTION #7: ASK THE QUESTION, "IS MY STRUCTURE OPTIMAL?"

Take inventory of what tax structure you have now.

How Is Your Business Structured?	
1	*Do you have a Sole Proprietorship, an LLC, an S corp, or a C corp? Ask yourself – "Do I know why I am an LLC?" If you do not know the answer, then make this question a to-do for your tax meeting with your service provider. Or simply contact Community CPA, and we have the answer.*

2	*Do you feel that you are paying too much money in taxes? If you literally borrow money to pay taxes, something is not right. Maybe your structure is unfitting. Or maybe your accounting needs to be looked at.*
3	*Look at your businesses; maybe one is making money and the other one is losing money. Could you combine them? That would save you at least 15% in taxes.*

Schedule an appointment with your CPA and ask if your tax structure fits you. If it does not, have the CPA help you elect a different structure. The fee for your CPA to make the election for your business may look small compared to what you will save in taxes!

CHAPTER 5

Do I Need a Partner?

REASONS FOR PARTNERSHIPS

In business, a partner could be a real person being a partner or a company acting as a partner.

From a money standpoint, being a partner means you would be in joint ownership and share profit or loss of the operation. Having a partner does not mean that you are a partnership company which would file a partnership return. A partner could be a percentage shareholder of your company. You may not have a partnership, but you have a corporation which has many shareholders.

A partner is simply the person who is doing the business together with you and holds ownership together with you. The ownership can either be presented in term of "membership units" or "number of shares."

People become business partners for many reasons. Maybe one partner is an immigrant from the Country of the Hand and the other is an immigrant from the Country of the Heart. One is lacking the skill to do a certain part of the business. The other one is lacking warmth towards people and cannot get hold of clients.

By now, if you have gone through the reflections for the first chapter, you should know what passport you hold to migrate to the Land of Business. It would be essential to know what passport your partners are holding. Business immigrants with different passports would make up the most effective partnership team. In fact you must have all three types of immigrants to make a business successful – those from the Countries of the Hand, Heart, and Head.

If you simply cannot find partners, then you will find them as your employees. Having them participate in the work is more important than whether they are your partner or not.

Maybe you feel that you need a partner who has cash to invest in the business. That is a valid reason. Many real estate partnerships are formed this way.

But consider your partner carefully. Does your potential partner bring problems to the deal that will be bigger than his investment? Does your partner have the same values and drive as you? Can you do this business alone without taking on a partner?

Listen to this good advice by Harris E. DeLoach, Jr., President and CEO of Sonoco: "I have found that the biggest successes and failures in business are most often determined by whether or not the right people are in the right jobs. You can have the best strategy, but it has no value without the right people to execute it. Conversely, if you have the wrong strategy but the right people, they will correct it. The right people truly do build businesses."[24]

PARTNERING FOR SKILL

A partner can bring a skill you need. If you are looking for a skill set, you probably want someone from the Country of the Hand. Maybe you are new to the business, and you need someone to teach you how to do a certain kind of work. Maybe you are growing so much that you need someone to take over a special area. This is one situation where a partner can be valuable.

HUA HUA AND JOHN:
A PARTNER BRINGS SKILLS

In some cases, you would need a partner because you do not have the set of skills you need for your business. For instance, Hua Hua started an online selling company that was doing great. Then, logistics and inventory control became a real labor-intensive area. Computerizing the process became a real need.

THE OFFER

She had a brother who at the time worked in a logistics company in China as the chief IT officer. Hua Hua decided to sponsor her brother through the H1 visa to come to the USA to work in her company. With her mom, Hua Hua mentioned that she would offer 10% of the company to her brother.

We started to work on the H1 application for John, but considering the risk of not getting the lottery and being rejected the visa, I asked Hua Hua to prepare for the worst in case John did not get the lottery and could not come.

She said, "We will try every year till he gets it. My brother is a genius in the logistics system design in China. If he comes, he can help me to move this company from 3-4 million dollars in sales to 30 and 40 million. Plus, I trust him and only him."

John got the H1 lottery on the first try, and the family came.

THE ADJUSTMENT

Moving from Shanghai, China to Ames, Iowa is not just a 14-hour time difference. It is a day and night difference in lifestyle and life situation. Once the honeymoon is over, issues start to bubble up.

Hua Hua was only prepared to work with her brother; she did not realize that she would really need to work with her sister in law, too. Hua Hua also did not realize that the 10% ownership was literally for Fei rather than for John, as Fei intended to live and work like a 10% owner in a much more literal way.

It did not take long before Fei realized that John was working a lot more hours than when he was in China. When John went to work, she would be alone. With her visa status as H4, she could not legally work. She had been a schoolteacher back home. Life in China seemed to have a lot more sounds and commotions.

Here this empty apartment could get so empty and quiet, and she felt sick. She realized that she did not like the idea that her husband worked for his younger sister, and not just that, he worked even more hours than the time he was working in China. And he was not apologetic toward her like he used to be.

They fought a lot. I started seeing them coming to me separately.

THE APPOINTMENT

One day Fei came alone. On my calendar it said: "Fei from Ames to meet Ying – concerns of partnership." I have these nice, bright yellow, comfy chairs for my clients. Fei sat in the client chair at the other side of the table, brought her knees to her chest, and curled up. She was such a good-looking Chinese lady, but I could tell she was sad and uneasy.

She cleared her throat and said, "Ying, I don't want you to tell anyone that I came to see you. Ying, you know how much John gets paid. He works too much, and he is not getting paid enough."

When we applied for John's H1 visa for him, the prevailing wages for John's position were $80,000 a year. Hua Hua offered $100,000, and at that time I thought that was pretty generous. Of course, John was the brother. So I asked, "Why do you think the paycheck is too low?"

"Well, I cannot work now, and he is not making enough to cover my pay in China. He works a lot more now than before." She started to get upset. "He is 10% owner, but I did not see anything special coming to him, and I think he is better off to be just employee and ask for more money."

Before I could think of a better way to explain things to her, she added, "I want out, and I want to go back to China."

"What would John think?" I asked.

She said, "John will do what I ask him to do; we both will go back to China."

I knew exactly where Fei was coming from, and I did not blame her. She did not understand Hua Hua's business struggle at all, and she could not occupy herself with things to do. So she started to cause issues. She also did not understand the culture of American companies. For small businesses, ownership equals "working hard with no place to complain." Ownership also means "getting paid last when there is leftover."

The Solution

I took the next few minutes with Fei to explain to her about her work status, the time of company distribution, and the uncertainty in Hua Hua's business. And most important, I explained the American way of compensating – how fair compensation stacked up with other companies in the same position. I even pulled out the Department of Labor prevailing wages report to show her. I think she walked away knowing that Hua Hua was fair to her husband and that her husband's work would bring a good future to the company, which in turn would benefit her through distribution. That was something she had yet to see at the year end.

For Hua Hua, I recommended her to ask her sister-in-law to come to the workplace and see what everybody did and how the business operated. Perhaps she could come up with some ideas to contribute to the wellbeing of the family business. Fei wasn't really working at the company as she needed to comply with the immigration regulation on H4. Later on, I learned that Fei gave some refreshing, artistic ideas to improve the shipping department's packaging with an amazing personal touch to the packages that went out to the first-time customers.

Bringing John and Fei to join the company turned out to be a good decision. Anne Beiler, Founder and CEO of Auntie Anne's, Inc., has said: "Keep going, gather good people around you to do what you can't, and focus on your gift."[25] That is just what Hua Hua did.

Yes, family drama is a huge issue in partnership. Someone once told me that if you want to get rid of your friend or destroy your family, be in business together. At Community CPA, we understand family dynamics.

Hua Hua's family literally was on the path to have great and bigger issues, but the growth of the company took a lot of pressure out of this relationship. Also, good accountants like us would help, too.

DONALD TRUMP: PARTNER FOR SKILL

You remember the Commodore Hotel, which Trump planned to gut and rebuild? The Commodore Hotel made Trump's reputation as a developer. The Commodore Hotel was in a good location, very close to Grand Central Station. But it was in bad shape. It didn't get very many guests because it looked so bad.

Trump knew how he wanted the place to look. In the middle of fancy old buildings, he wanted a mirror surface. He was excited at how it would reflect the historic buildings nearby. He pushed his ideas through the city planning committee and got to work.

GETTING THE HYATT

But Trump had never run a hotel before. He wanted a partner to operate it for him to make up for the skills he lacked. He chose Hyatt because he admired the hotel brand. He liked how they did things.

Trump knew an executive at Hyatt, and he sold the man on the possibilities in the Commodore. But he could never get a commitment from him. That executive seemed unable to follow through on arrangements. Finally, one Hyatt employee pointed Trump towards someone higher up in the organization. Things started moving as soon as Trump contacted the man with the power. "Suddenly it dawned on me why my deals kept coming apart: if you're going to make a deal of any significance, you have to go to the top."[26]

Trump got his deal to have Hyatt be his partner. Hyatt would run the Commodore. Construction went well, and when the new hotel opened, many people began to stay there. The new hotel was clean, beautiful, and luxurious. Trump was very proud of what he had done.

Managing Trump

Trump wanted to remain involved in the day-to-day operations of the Hyatt-run Commodore Hotel, but the Hyatt people didn't like his interruptions and opinions. His wife would go through the lobby finding things that needed to be done. The manager complained to Hyatt, who talked to Trump.

When Trump refused to be less vocal, the Hyatt executives hired a new manager – one who went to Trump constantly about the smallest decisions. The manager was even Eastern European, like Trump's wife; so he had similar ideas.

Eventually Trump got tired of being pestered with details and told the manager to stop bothering him. "What the manager did was the perfect ploy, because he got what he wanted not by fighting but by being positive and friendly and solicitous."[27]

Trump has had an up and down relationship with partners. Like any Head person, he likes partners who make him money and don't cause him problems. If someone doesn't do what they say or if someone costs him money, Trump will have a problem with that person.

He could benefit from learning the ways of a Heart person. But in the area of real estate, Trump already knows the skills of a Hand person. So he embodies the business immigrant from the Countries of the Hand and the Head. He looks at every little detail of his properties. But he doesn't spend any time to be a person from the Country of the Heart. That's what drove the Hyatt manager crazy! Because he is from the Country of the Heart.

PARTNERING FOR INVESTMENT

Maybe you have all the skill you need to run your business; you just need cash. This could be true of a chef who needs a building and kitchen equipment. It could be true of a therapist who needs an office to set up an independent practice. If you need a partner for investment, listen to these stories.

Jose and Eric: A Partner Brings Capital

When Jose first moved into his warehouse for his equipment repair company, the landlord was asking for $5,400 a month rent. Jose did not have that much money to spare, and most importantly, he was not used to spending a big chunk on rent like that. However, the building was truly the most perfect one for him. It even had a ramp loading zone so that larger equipment could be pulled in from the ramp into the warehouse.

What Do You Need?

Jose came to me and asked me to help him talk to the landlord. The landlord, Eric, was a second-generation farmer who had just inherited a large sum of land and the warehouse from his father.

Eric had a lot of equity but very little cash.

Eric wanted to get cash rent, and he also liked the business Jose was doing. Jose liked the location and warehouse, but he was not sure whether he could afford paying so much in the beginning or whether he wanted to lose so much of his cash flow.

So I helped to structure a partnership: The lease was $5,400 a month. However, if the lease amount was not paid timely, each month of lease payment due would result in a conversion of .16% ownership of Jose's business to Eric's warehouse company. If a year rent was not paid, Eric's warehouse company would get 2% of equity in Jose's company. For 10 years, Eric's warehouse company would have 20% of the ownership.

They both jumped at the opportunity.

Everybody Wins

Jose got a partner. It helped him to get started in the new location without worrying about the $5,400 monthly rent. If this rent was not paid, he only ended up converting the rent amount to the proceeds of selling shares. That would have a very minimal tax consequence compared to borrowing money to pay rent.

For Eric, the young farmer, he loved Jose's operation, and he also understood the business. He did not mind getting involved at all.

ELON MUSK: THE ULTIMATE INVESTOR

Elon Musk started his business life with very safe partnerships: his brother and his cousins. Family ties made those partnerships ones in which he could feel safe and be himself. Musk's first experience with an outside partnership happened at Zip2.

Zip2 was supposed to merge with CitySearch, a company that was creating a similar product. Musk opposed the merger, but the board went through with it and removed him as CEO. Musk had learned a hard lesson about losing power.[28]

No Confidence

That may explain why Musk worked so hard to keep control of his company when X.com merged with PayPal. But Musk was more tied to X.com than PayPal, and he wanted to keep doing things his way. One of the leaders of PayPal, Peter Thiel, resigned over the decisions Musk was making.

The employees and executives were unhappy about some of the decisions, like not being allowed to use Linux software. The website was also not keeping up with demand. So when Musk left for his honeymoon in Australia, the executives delivered letters of no confidence to the board, which fired Musk as CEO and called Peter Thiel to take his place.[29]

That decision was a slap in the face. Musk decided that he would be much more careful with partners.

Young Boy, No.

When he was starting SpaceX, he went on a trip to Russia to see if space-supply companies would sell him missiles. At the end of one meeting, the Russian executives "sat there and looked at him…and said something like, 'Young boy. No.' They also intimated that he didn't have the money."[30] So Musk got up and walked out. He wasn't going to partner with anyone who didn't respect him.

Elon Musk was in charge of SpaceX when he started it. No partnership worries there. When he and an employee disagreed, the employee could leave.

Chairman Musk

But Tesla grew out of a company started by two engineers, Martin Eberhard and Marc Tarpenning. When they wanted investors, Elon Musk gave them so much that he got to be chairman of the company. So the men were partners. But they did not agree on a lot.

Eberhard, who was the CEO, did not have a car background. He arranged for supplies and manufacturing that lost the company money. He did not like or understand the financial software used by Tesla, and as a result the board did not know how far in debt they were. Musk asked the board to replace Eberhard as CEO, and it did. Eberhard was bitter about the loss of his position.[31] Tarpenning left much later on good terms because he felt he was finished with his time at the company.[32]

Elon Musk has had a hard time with partnership. He will probably always do best at a company where he can be in complete control. Like any Hand person, he focuses deeply on the work in front of him. Big financial strategies and other people's personalities take second place.

FRANCIS AND LEO: FLIPPERS

Francis and Leo were two partners in the real estate business. Francis was in his later 20s, and Leo was about to retire and in his 60s. They met at the local tequila bar, where most subcontractors would go to drink after work.

FLIPPING HOUSES

Francis noticed Leo a couple of times. Leo wore expensive outfits and was a bit off tone from this crowd in the bar. But a couple of Latino folks would say Hola to him as if they all knew him. So Francis decided to say Hi one of these days to him.

After a couple of drinks and a couple of hours hot chat, Leo put down a $250K investment, and Francis identified a couple of run-down homes. They were going to partner together to flip houses.

Leo just wanted to get a return on his investment and would

not get involved in actual labor. In fact, he just wanted to stay in the bar and find more people like Francis to do more deals. He had already been so successful in finding partners, that would be his eighth partnership with a new partner.

PAYING TAXES

Francis was so talented in fixing and interior design. He used the $250k to buy three broken houses; within 18 months, all three were sold. After covering all the material expenses and guaranteed payment to Francis, as he was the one who did the job, the net profit was $98k. $46k went to Leo – an 18% rate of return.

The benefit for Leo to be this kind of partner was that his gains were only subject to income tax, not self-employment tax. That was a solid 15% saving on tax - $6,900 tax saving by being Leo.

For Francis, the $46K would be taxed both on income and on self-employment tax. On top of the guaranteed payment, he needed to pay both taxes as well. Yes, when you made money, paying tax was like the seal of your victory – in a most authoritative way – "I paid my taxes."

My dad once said to me: "In China, the proudest matter is to pay the Communist Party due (you are a Party member), but for USA, the proudest matter is to pay taxes (you are a taxpayer)."

THE HOTEL COUPLE: NO SWEAT

Pretend your partnership made $100,000 in sales, and then it spent $96,000. So you only end up with $4,000 in profit for all the partners in the partnership. This $4,000 gets split among partners and ends up at each partner's personal checking account.

THE SWEAT TAX

This $4,000 profit will go to each one of you in the partnership. You will pay income taxes on it just like the schedule C income. You pay under the personal tax rate, and you also pay self-employment tax.

"Whoa, whoa – okay, I understand that I do schedule C; I pay income tax and self-employment tax. Now you just said that if I do a partnership, I'm still gonna pay income tax and self-employment tax?"

Yes. Correct. There's only one exception. Sometimes when you have a partnership, you're the one doing the work, and the other guy just puts in the money. Maybe he gives you $20,000. The person who doesn't work and just gives you money is called a passive partner. That person does not have to pay self-employment tax on the K1 you give to him

See, self-employment tax works this way. You pay self-employment tax on income you get as long as you worked and you sweated. It is a sweat tax. If you don't sweat, you're just giving your money and walking around watching. Then you pay income tax on the partnership income, and you should not pay self-employment tax.

HOTEL SAVINGS

We have a husband and wife client who run hotels, they are Snaha and James. James and Snaha own the hotels under a partnership. They usually, at the end of the year, have a half a million-dollar profit that goes to their joint 1040 tax return. Before they came to us, they paid income tax and self-employment tax on the income from the partnership.

So when they came to our firm, I asked the lady, "So, what type of work do you do in the hotel?"

She answered, "I don't go there. It's just my husband's job. I never go to the hotels."

What does Snaha's answer tell you? She never sweats, and she does not work at the hotels. She should never need to pay self-employment tax. And there is 15% of half a million. We're talking about $75,000. We save $37,500 every year for her.

This is an example of how your partnership can be structured. If both you and your partner don't sweat, you should never put yourself in a situation where both of you are paying self-employment tax.

The Home Office

A partner can be an asset for you, but he or she can easily turn out to be a liability. Partner wisely, and never rush to an attorney to solve partner issues. Try your CPA first; if not, come to talk to me.

Bitter Air

Sometimes I sit there and listen to both sides of the stories from both partners. My heart goes out to them. I almost never see this type of pain as necessary. It is a waste of energy and time. But at that moment of anger, folks have energy to waste.

I feel the pain for them. I allow that bitter air to evaporate; it's okay to let out the steam. And then when I sense the opportunity of the dark silence between them, I introduce a way to deal with the issue. A lot of times, it is simply working through the numbers with both parties.

One time, two partners were arguing about home office reimbursement expenses that were paid from the partnership bank account. One partner had a bigger home; so the reimbursement check was $2,500. These expenses were higher. The other one had a small condo and nearly no expenses; he only got $120 reimbursement.

The partner with $2,500 house reimbursement was upset. As the expenses were split 50% 50%, she did not get the full deduction of the home office expense. Therefore, her K1 income would be higher than what it really should be.

The other partner was dumbfounded about the issue, as he did not even get what she gets at the first place. He only got $120, which was "a little less than $2,500," as he said. The fight got elevated to my office.

TECHNICAL SOLUTION

I said, "Let's not deduct the home office in the partnership return at all."

"You mean just to pay more taxes?" one said angrily.

"No," I said. "to be fair, you take your respective home office expenses to your own 1040 Schedule E under supplemental income and expenses." They both were wordless for a long while.

Literally there is a technical solution to save this fight. Knowing how is as important as being compassionate. This is where I advise "finding a technical solution before drawing an emotional conclusion."

Partnership comes with a high risk in joint efforts. Only choose to be in partnership when you know the joint venture is going to benefit the business in such way that it would offset your emotion of disliking each other. It is guaranteed that you must learn to accept each other.

Yes, do not forget to package your acceptance to each other before getting together.

PROBLEMS WITH PARTNERS

A partnership can start off doing well, and with time problems develop through bad communication or business struggles. The reality about business is that all businesses struggle. Some struggle with music in heart and some struggle with resentment in emotions.

Maybe one partner felt he was underpaid by the signed partnership agreement, and driven by that "unfair" feeling, he started to steal money or not do the work he should do for the joint business venture. Or a partnership could have problems waiting to happen from the beginning because the partners did not know each other very well. They entered a joint venture thinking, *As long as we make money, we will be okay.*

The reality is that there will never be enough money to make. The partnership will come down to being fair again and again, whether you make a dollar or make a million.

In business, it is important to know your partner's country of origin, know your own origin, understand the difference between each other, and communicate clearly and often. Deal with problems in the open, and do it as soon as you know about them. Bring your "hard-to-reconcile" problems to someone who you look up to. I am not an attorney, although at one time in my life I dreamed to be one, but I have helped many partners to solve partnership issues by simply talking together.

On the other hand, think of the problems that Elon Musk had in his partnerships. Sometimes the partnership just needs to dissolve. Sometimes the right partner in the beginning is not the right partner later on. Conceptually, we need to accept that to be a natural progress of a mature business.

PARTNERS IN TROUBLE

Many times the partner who helps you to start the business is not the partner who helps you to build the business venture. Some startup partners are suitable to work within a structure and thrive within the boundaries. But some are risk takers, and they have no boundaries.

One time I met two young men who were partners in a wholesale business. They were selling certain products to the end user; so a sales tax should be collected. I thought that would be very important for both of them to know. So I called them to my office for a meeting and provided an estimate of sales tax that should be collected and paid based on our study of their books.

One of them said: "Who does not make mistakes when they just started up a business? As long as I am not being caught, I do not want to know or care. If I get caught, I might already have money to pay it all up."

I could tell the other partner was thinking, and although he made no comment, he was not happy to hear his partner's comments.

Not long after, the "don't care" guy came back. He got audited by the sales tax folks, and he was angry. He told me that his partner left and reported him to the state. The business was in turmoil.

Obviously in this case their moral compass was different, and their risk tolerance level was apart. Partnering with people who do not operate life on the same wavelength will, sooner or later, create turmoil like this. Many partnerships dissolve when partners are facing challenges.

ECKHART TOLLE: CONSCIOUS PARTNERSHIP

Often times partners can have difficulties with one another that have nothing to do with facts about the company. It is not an issue of who did something wrong. It is just one person liking things done one way and another person liking things done another way.

EGO TRICKS

Eckhart Tolle has a good way to explain why these problems between people can happen. These problems happen because of the ego. The ego is the part of us that wants problems and fights so that we can win them. It is the part of us that wants to feel big, even if we make someone else feel small.

The ego uses many tricks to feed itself. It complains, holds grudges, and starts arguments for no reason. It creates enemies and chooses sides. It excludes others for the pleasure of choosing who belongs and who doesn't.[33]

When two partners in business have a problem, chances are that the ego of one or the other is very active. Maybe both. What can you do if you are having a problem with a business partner?

AWARENESS

The answer is that you can do nothing about the other person. You can only do something about you. And what you should do first is to become aware of any ego in you that is causing problems.

"If in the midst of negativity, you are able to realize, 'At this moment I am creating suffering for myself' it will be enough to raise you above the limitations of conditioned egoic states and reactions. It will open up infinite possibilities which come to you when there is awareness."[34]

Awareness guides your mind to solving problems, not to being right. Awareness can admit when you are wrong. Awareness can look at the other partner in friendship and acceptance, believing that there is a way forward.

Of course, some partners are so deeply caught in ego that the same problems arise again and again. In that case, I think that Eckhart Tolle would agree with dissolving the partnership. You are not required to spend your one valuable life tending to the suffering of an unconscious person.

COMMUNITY CPA PARTNERSHIP

I did not look for a partner when I started Community CPA. I did not need capital, as a professional services company has very little need to purchase anything big. I also did not feel that my skills needed to be supplemented by another partner. The fact was that I did not know a lot; for that reason, I felt that I knew it all.

My first encounter that completely diminished my ego occurred when I was 10 months into the practice. One of my clients came to me and showed me what his lawyer did for him in the formation of an LLC document. With the information he provided to me, looking at what was done, I made a judgement very quickly. "Your lawyer is wrong," I said.

My dear client rushed back to his lawyer and told him: "Ying said you are wrong." The lawyer reported me to the Supreme Court of Iowa for unauthorized practice of law.

Confused with how I got there and scared of the big charge on me, I planned to quit doing what I was doing. I did not understand what part of what I do was the law part and what was the CPA part. My husband, who is a mathematician, not lawyer, was a huge help to me when a thorough research was needed to combat the groundless claim.

The charge on me was dismissed with the work Steve did on my behalf.

So I have a partner. A partner who is from the Country of the Head. A partner not just in business but in all of life.

Over the years at Community CPA, I continued on my path to build an efficient compensation model and lay ground for a profit-sharing partnership, where staff members in our team will share the growth of the firm through compensation.

To run a successful practice under my leadership, I learned that I need people who are from the Country of the Hand and also the Country of the Head.

As myself, I am the business immigrant from the Country of the Heart. The combination of three is the essential element for business success. I have Steve, who fulfills one element, and I have come to realize with time that I actually hired my first partner from the Country of the Hand long before I knew what I was doing.

His name was Mo. He got things done with quality and precision. He led the firm to implement technologies so our work could be perfect with ease. Although he left the firm after 10 long years of service, what he had done had already become the culture of the firm. Staff members from the Country of the Hand are the movers, shakers, and contributors to our fast-growing CPA practice in this country.

For a professional firm like Community CPA, the intrinsic value resides with people, and collectively we are the assets of this practice. There would be no other way but finding a method to reward professional behaviors timely and fairly across the board.

In terms of the traditional partnerships those older generation professional firms are having, I consider them the outdated model.

The equity of the firm is a placeholder for risks only. The fewer equity partners, the less spread of the risks.

When a professional firm got sued for millions, it was the equity partners who would take the risk. The rest of the profit-sharing staff members could never be affected.

So in essence, every member of our team is a partner to Community CPA. Staff at Community CPA are not employees. They are partners in this grand, big goal – the minority-operated, professional CPA firm that holds KPMG as a standard for our quality of work and our prosperity.

As one wise leader has said: "The finest, most successful people I have met are resolutely positive and optimistic, always believing they will achieve their goals. There is nothing more inspiring and stimulating than being in the company of optimists."[35]

That speaks my mind.

REFLECTION #8: SHOULD I HAVE A PARTNER?

The following reflection is for someone who does not yet have a partner. Maybe you are considering a proposal from someone who wants to be your partner. Maybe you are just feeling unsure about running a business by yourself and you want someone to share risk.

	PARTNER CONSIDERATIONS
1	Write down a list of the tasks that need to be done by somebody in your business. These tasks might include things like payroll and tax preparation, shipping and distribution, daily accounting, cleaning the workspace, creating product, advertising, and serving customers.
2	Beside each task on this list, put a checkmark beside those things that you are good at doing. Now, look at the rest. Do you need a partner to do the other things? Can you hire these tasks out by the job? Can you learn to do the things you are not good at doing?
3	Take a hard and honest look at your finances and your business plan. (If you do not have a business plan already, stop reading this book and contact me!) There are many resources online to teach you how to complete this necessary preparation. According to your business plan, do you have the resources to hire, or do you need someone coming to bring a large sum of money or to bring a set of skills?
4	Carefully consider the partner who is offering to bring the investment in cash. Is this someone you know well? Is this someone you like? Do you agree with this person on how the business should be run? Is this person going to micro-manage you from now on because he or she provided you the money?
5	If having a partner is not likely the option, could you start a smaller version of your business and save profits to make the investment yourself? Could you investigate a loan from your bank or from the Small Business Administration? How important is it to have a partner?

REFLECTION #9: FINDING NEMO – THE BEST MATCH

The following are six business activities under which all others fall and which different types of business immigrants are naturally skilled to work. Where do your strengths lie? Consider finding the right partner. If you are from the Land of the Heart, finding someone from the Land of the Hand and the Head would be optimal. As you can see, business immigrants from different Lands would have different skillful areas.

THE 6 MAIN BUSINESS ACTIVITIES & WHICH PASSPORTS SPECIALIZE IN EACH			
	HEART	HAND	HEAD
BUDGETING		x	
ACCOUNTING & AUDITING			x
MARKETING			x
SALES	x		
OPERATIONS & SUPLLY CHAIN		x	
CUSTOMER SERVICE	x		

REFLECTION #10: I HATE MY PARTNER

This Reflection is for someone who already has a partner in business. But the relationship is not working out. The partnership is so toxic, and you feel like just walking away.

	HATING YOUR PARTNER
1	*Write down on a piece of paper why you became a partner with him to begin with. You may say: "Well, it was his idea to do this business." Or you maybe think: "We knew each other, and we both did not have a job so…" Just write down the reasons.*
2	*Write down what changed so the partnership is no longer a good idea. You may think: "While he is lazy, I work more hours." Or you may say: "He has to be stealing money as we are making much less now." Just write it down.*
3	*With the first two writings, you would sort out why you hated your partner. Can you walk away? Or do you want to walk away? If No is your answer, then go on:*
4	*Write down what needs to happen so you would feel OK with this partner. For instance, you might say: "If he comes in earlier each day, or if our business can make more money."*
5	*Next to your wishes from above, give a time line to get the wish fulfilled. For instance: "Tomorrow I will bring a cup of coffee with me to my partner and just tell him that he needs to come in as early as I come in, and we will work together more." On items like: "I wish the business is doing better," share that wish with your partner, and come up with some ideas together.*
6	*Be alone somewhere you are not rushed or crowded, and give yourself time to think and to write. Then answer the following questions. Be honest, noting good and bad qualities. Nothing is ever all good or all bad.*

Keep in mind in partnership there is no right or wrong; there is only good or better. Sometimes good is the best for the partnership, and better can mean the end of the partnership.

Eckhart said: "Let life happen to you, and do not judge."

CHAPTER 6

Do I Need a Loan?

WE ARE ALL BUSINESS IMMIGRANTS

As a startup company, if you personally do not have any savings, it is very natural to think: "Where do I find capital?"

You may be thinking after the last chapter, "That is easy. If I do not have the money, I will go find a partner." That is certainly an option, and I think that it is a better option than borrowing from a bank. Just make sure you follow my advice about partnerships!

Whatever you do to start your business, things will work much better if you plan carefully. Archie W. Dunham, Chairman of ConocoPhillips, said: "I received some good advice in the United States Marine Corps, something called the Five Ps: 'Prior planning prevents poor performance.' One reason why the Marines are so successful is the thoroughness with which they plan: they think about alternatives, they anticipate what could go wrong, and they provide for contingencies."[36]

There are many ways to start a business. The only wrong way is to start without planning. That way will lead to expensive mistakes and maybe the loss of what you already have. But there is good news! This chapter will help you to plan and think about options.

STARTING WITHOUT LOANS

Gerard J. Arpey, President and CEO of American Airlines advises: "Borrow money when you can, not when you need to."[37] If you are in desperate need, you cannot decide the terms of your loan agreement. Waiting and saving are always best. Then you can borrow when you are able to do so more safely.

Starting a business without loans is very hard. You will have to think again about what you really need to begin. You will have to think creatively about how you can get what you need. You will have to make your money stretch.

But this is not impossible to do. I have done this, and so have many clients. I almost think that immigrants to the USA are better equipped to start a business here without borrowing because they are used to doing with so little.

You say, "Tighten your belt; cut some corners," to a US-born American, and that person may be thinking, "I have to get less expensive cable TV. Maybe I can get a different car insurance or stop my gym membership."

You say the same thing to a first-generation immigrant from an Asian or African or South American country, and that person will probably think, "We can eat meat only one time per week. And my shoes can last another six months if I glue the soles back on."

It is a totally different mindset.

There are also differences to how a business immigrant from the Countries of the Hand, Heart, and Head will think about getting money without asking the bank. I have learned these kinds of differences from my clients, my role models, and my own life.

How Jose Started

Jose did not have money when he came to this country. You remember that he mowed his first lawn for a few dollars. Then he learned on the job how to fix the equipment he needed to mow lawns. He had no money to learn these skills.

Now Jose has a heavy equipment warehouse where he is doing machinery fixing. From Lifting Tongs to Spreader Beams, the value of these kinds of equipment is over half a million dollars each. But did Jose take out a loan to buy these things?

No. He financed this equipment through the growth of the company. When the company was a startup company, he had his hands and handy tools. Sometimes he borrowed a client's tools.

He did not get any loans. Remember, he could not get any loans as he had no credit history in this country, and he had an ITIN number instead of a social security number. Because loans were not an option, Jose found another way to get the tools he needed.

And this way of growing and expanding is very natural to a Hand person like Jose. He is concerned with the work in front of him, right? So he finds a way to meet immediate needs with the resources at hand (his own tools or a client's tools), and he waits and saves to buy better ones.

For one of his large lifters, Jose needed this equipment so badly. He went to the dealership a couple of times. The salesperson got to know him and told him, "My boss might let you take that, and you can pay back in 10 installments."

So Jose took the equipment back to the shop, used it, and paid in full within 6 installments. I asked: "Oh, so you got a loan?"

"What loan? Promised to pay in 10 payments."

So it was not a loan from the bank. It was equipment financing that allowed Jose to use the product first and then pay it in full over time.

How I Started

For Jose, it is luxury to be able to borrow. "Borrowing means you have a social security number." My heart aches when he says that. It is from his point of view.

Being able to borrow from the bank also means you have resources.

When you first start borrowing, you will soon realize that you must have something first before you can borrow. Banks do not give away money for nothing with nothing on the back end to secure the loan.

The concept of borrowing is a negative term for most of the Chinese from China at my age. I had a hard time borrowing anything from anyone. If I did not have the money, that means I would not do what I want to do.

Remember, in college I did not have a quarter to make a phone call! So I would just walk and be late. I would definitely be skipping pleasures for lack of money. Sometimes I skipped meals for money.

So the way I started Community CPA was to measure what my business could do to avoid borrowing. I did not have material needs like tools or equipment. With my knowledge and a home computer, I could start to do the work.

I did not rent an office. I used my home office for the first five years of the business. And during that time, I was working a full-time job to make ends meet and also cover the other business expenses.

But opportunity showed up, and Peter Keobunta offered me an office next to his fish store without my needing to pay 12 months' rent. What a generous gift! Peter said to me: "Come to Des Moines, Ying, we need you here." Five years after moving onto 2nd Avenue, I left my full-time job and made Community CPA my only work. I did not leave my full-time job until the day I knew I could survive without borrowing.

When it was time to grow, I planned ahead. I measured my spending to make sure I could afford to hire an employee with the money I made. Until I could, I would just do the work myself without hiring anyone. I grew slowly and expanded carefully. I gathered enough community support before I moved to the next step.

Can you see how Community CPA is coming from a business immigrant from the Country of the Heart? I gave my time to Peter and Meg with no thought of return, only gladness that I could help. Then my generosity came back to me in the form of office space and service income. I credit the success wholeheartedly to the community where I belong. Heart people will naturally look to friendships and other relationships for help starting a business.

THE CREDIT CARD SHUFFLE

In the year 2003, I met three brothers who had started a business in a very unusual way. All three of them were foreign students who were about to graduate from a local college. "We want to start a business together," they told me. They were Head people, and they believed in the principle that money makes money. They put their minds to finding a way to get some seed money.

This seed money came from one credit card with a $600 credit limit. That is a very low credit limit. Can you imagine starting a business on so little? But that is what they did.

Because they were foreign students, their English was not very good. They did not want to get into doing much face-to-face customer service. So they started an online selling business. They knew that if they sold basic necessities, people would not need much customer service as long as the price was low and the process was timely.

After researching what to sell, they settled on office supplies: packages, pens, and papers. They bought these supplies at very low prices by shopping worldwide, and they paid the purchases by using the credit card, which they planned to pay in 30 days. Their customers paid them up front before getting the product, and the students used these payments to pay off the credit card constantly, before interest charges could accumulate.

Then they got more credit cards as their credit history was getting populated with timely payment records and credit score going up. By the end of 12 months, they were shuffling 12 credit cards! They moved their money around from one card to another, constantly moving and keeping track so that there was no interest. It was like a game. But this game got them $660,000 in sales and $55,000 in credit by the end of that first year.

They could not work for wages as they were all foreign students; so there was no payroll for the students. But they hired fellow students to package and ship the office supplies, paying payroll to the packagers.

At the same time, the three brothers took advantage of the company growth and applied for an H1 visa for each one of them. Their status matter was resolved. They no longer had any issue about working in their own business.

They focused on growing the business.

Ten years later, the company had grown from its Iowa startup location to have branches in California and Malaysia. It did $7 million in sales per year. No loans, and in fact the bank offered loans to the students. In unison they said: No.

Can you see that this startup could only have come from the imaginations of Head people? Money was a game to them. They made up rules to that game that would let them win.

See? The kind of business was not important. The clients were not the focus. The point of the game was to expand that $600 credit limit up and up, and the game worked.

THE STINKY OFFICE

For the big businesses everyone knows, like Tesla and SpaceX, Elon Musk did not need loans. He made so much money off his earlier businesses that he put his profits into new companies. To look at Elon Musk starting a business like an ordinary person, you need to look at his first startup: Zip2.

When Elon and Kimball Musk started Zip2, their father Errol

gave them $28,000 to help them out. This was not a loan they would need to pay back. Their father wanted to see them succeed.

The brothers used that money to rent a small office, get software, and purchase equipment like computers. The money was soon gone, and then the brothers got creative. They called Navteq, a computer mapping company, and it gave them technology for free. They ran a line to a downstairs neighbor and paid him to use his Internet.

They slept in the office and showered in the YMCA. Without a kitchen, they ate cheap fast food. The toilet backed up sometimes. That was a stinky office!

When they had an apartment, they used one room to gain an intern who would work for room and board. Slowly, they made more money and improved their living situation bit by bit. But they did not live well until they sold that first company.[38] Even then, much of the profit went straight into another business, not into a bank account.

Anyone who looks at Elon Musk the millionaire now and thinks that he has it easy needs to look at his early days. He hasn't always lived in a mansion. Part of the reason he has so much now is that he was willing to work so hard in that stinky office! His journey to success is very much like the other person from the Country of the Hand, Jose.

STARTING WITH LOANS

I like the advice of William T. Monahan, Chairman and CEO of Imation Corporation. "No is the best word in the business vocabulary. If you are not willing to say no to bad business, no to poor deals, and no to poor returns in order to focus on better opportunities, you cannot win…Free is the worst word in business. Free offers, free samples, free trials – all have the value that the customer paid – zero."[39]

We cannot start to talk about loans without talking about these two wonderful words. Learn to love the word no. Learn to love telling yourself the word no, and you will build your savings quickly. Learn to love telling others no, and you will avoid bad situations.

Also, learn to shun the word free, especially in regard to loans. Monahan is exactly right. Loans are not free. They come with a price.

Some of my readers will believe that you must start a business with loans. There are other places you can get loans besides the bank. One of those places is from investors.

I will show you why an investor is so much better than a bank loan.

INVESTOR VERSUS LOAN

Certainly in some startup companies, it is essential to have money to invest in pricey equipment. Without it, the business does not exist. A shipping company needs trucks. A restaurant needs a commercial kitchen and dining space. A construction company needs land, equipment, and materials, as well as a crew.

In these kinds of situations, I would consider an investor versus a loan. The fundamental differences between investors and bankers are:

- Investors can be taken in as shareholders or members so that the timing and amount of their payback is controlled by the business owner.
- Especially if you start a company with a private placement type of funding structure, the payout is in the future. Investors could end up not getting the money back if your startup did not survive. It is part of the normal risk of being an opportunity-centric investor.
- A bank loan has an amortization schedule. Payout is immediate. If you default, the bank can call the whole loan due

in one day, leaving you with no cash to operate. They have your checking account, too.

- When you get the bank loan, you also sign a personal guarantee. That is an enforceable paper when you are in default. The bank will not hesitate to foreclose your personal residence if you do not pay the loan payment on time.

Remember when I said that we would talk more about banks not lending money for nothing? Now we are going to talk. If you are going to start a business, you are an optimistic person. You believe that your business will grow and succeed. You believe that you will meet your obligations. That is good!

But you must balance your optimism with reality. Some businesses fail, even when the owners work really hard. The owners do everything right, and still the business fails. If that happens to you, did you gamble something you can afford to lose?

A bank loan for a business is a gamble, like rolling the dice on a Las Vegas game. Instead of chips on the table, you have your home, your parents' home, your car, your parents' car, or something else valuable. The bank will not lend to you unless you name something valuable that it can take and sell if you do not pay.

If you lose your gamble, can you afford to lose that house or that car? Consider before you borrow.

THE OIL AND GAS BUST

Donald Trump knew someone in the oil and gas business. This person came to him with an investment opportunity that sounded really solid. The friend assured Trump that he would make his money back several times over.

Wanting to help out a friend, Trump agreed to the investment. But then he started to have second thoughts. He did not know anything about this business. Up until this point, he had invested only in property. That was something he knew well. He knew the risks. He knew the right questions to ask.

But in the oil and gas business, he would have to spend a lot of time learning the business before he knew what questions to ask. There was room for error and for foolish mistakes. Trump did not like that kind of risk.

So he backed out of the oil and gas investment, even though he was sorry to disappoint his friend. Soon after he backed out, his friend's company went bankrupt. All the investors lost their money.

Trump said: "That experience taught me a few things. One is to listen to your gut, no matter how good something sounds on paper. The second is that you're generally better off sticking with what you know. And the third is that sometimes your best investments are the ones you don't make."[40]

We can learn a lesson from this story as businesspeople seeking investment. We should go to people or to the bankers who know about our kind of business. Donald Trump's friend should have gone to someone who knew about oil and gas, not just to a rich guy. Someone who knows our business is someone who is much more likely to stick with us.

So be wise in choosing the partner you approach for loan or investment.

BANK BULLY

I met a business owner who started a nonprofit without a penny in his pocket. His donor even paid the formation fee for the nonprofit. Through his leadership, the Department of Labor funded the nonprofit with a $2.5 million grant to help with diversity workforce development.

The way this nonprofit worked with the government is that the nonprofit would help the minority businesses and keep records of what it spent for a month. On the monthly basis, the nonprofit would submit a reimbursement request to the government. The government would pay the nonprofit back for the cost.

This grant was reimbursement in nature. The nonprofit always struggled as they could never come ahead. They had no surplus cash flow to operate. Whenever the reimbursement arrived, it was not enough to meet the expenses for the next business project. The nonprofit wanted to help the businesses in need. So it went to the bank and borrowed funds to cover the timing shortage in cash flow.

The funding protocol was such an un-business-friendly process! The organization struggles, and at times, everything had to wait patiently for the government money to arrive.

So the bank loan was in default from time to time. Very quickly, the bank lost its patience and closed the bank account where the federal funds would come in. The organization was forced to close once the bank closed the account.

The organization might have been able to survive with a better management in cash flow, but without the bank being in the center of its game. It shut down the bank account; that then ended the time for this nonprofit.

If I were on that board, I would hire a CPA firm to manage cash flow instead of getting a bank loan. Plan ahead so that your cash flow covers your needs, with a little extra put aside for emergencies. Borrow only when you can easily pay it back timely.

EFFICIENCY

But maybe you see no other way. You have no investor, and you cannot start small like Jose and I did. So you have to borrow from the bank.

The money you get from the bank must be used very efficiently. Otherwise, you lose. Normally when you spend a dollar on raw materials, your product sells for 5 dollars. If that one dollar for materials is from your own operating fund, not borrowed money, you have four dollars of profit.

But if this one dollar is a borrowed dollar, you have to add interest expense, which increases your costs. Assume that your interest is 5%. Your one dollar of raw material is actually $1.05. Can you survive when you make $3.95 profit instead of $4.00 profit?

What will you have to do in order to survive on less profit? Will you have to sell something that is not as good? Will you have to take the missing money from your payroll? The money has to come from somewhere.

Borrowed money is not efficient in most start up business cases.

THE EFFICIENCY LOAN

In most cases, yes, a loan is not efficient. But in some cases, a loan will guarantee a specific, predictable savings to an already thriving business. That specific savings will pay back the loan quickly and surely. Then is the time to make an exception. Just make sure that you start with a good plan.

One fast food restaurant client came with her restaurant's year-end financial statements about 10 months ago. She had mixed feelings about her business. The restaurant produced good sales. But for whatever reason, it had a very small profit margin. She wanted to know why.

I asked: "Is there a reason why you have such a high payroll amount? What is the average hourly rate do you pay?"

"$13.00 an hour and not much overtime pay."

"For a fast food restaurant, the payroll to sales ratio should be right around 25-30%. Do you know why you spent more money on payroll?"

"No, we are busy. I did not pay myself yet."

"Is your space efficient? Do you consider your workflow smooth? Do you have a large distance to cover between cooked food and customer?"

"Ying, you are so right! We have a huge space in the kitchen.

The stoves are way in the back, and the cashiers are way in the front. How did you know? Did you go to my place already?" The client paused a little and said: "I don't think you did. How did you know I have that issue?"

The next day, I went to visit the client's restaurant. I walked the space in the kitchen, sat down, and had my lunch while observing the workflow. I provided the plan to the business owner on the spot:

Take off the current wall and build a long serving counter, so cooked meal will be on the counter with a number. Customers pick up their own food, eliminating the person who stands there shouting the number for pick up.

Push the whole long counter close to the kitchen stove area – eliminating the busboy running between cashier (pick up the order) and cook.

Move cashier to one end of the counter; cashier will turn to left and leave the order ticket on the counter where cooks can look at it and cook without needing to hold out a hand to receive the order, saving cooks time.

Make kitchen an open concept so customer can see foods are being cooked there – so long wait can be more understandable when the kitchen is looking busy.

Construction cost will be around $35K and can be covered by savings from payroll - 2 full-time salaries equivalent - $35,000

Six months after the renovation was done, the business owner emailed back to Dan, who is the operations manager of the firm:

"Dan, how are you? Just want to set a time to meet Ying again this year. Recall that she made recommendation for me to change, and I did it. I know it was the right thing to do, but I did not know how much an impact it would have on the business to make this change. I have just started on the new workflow for about 3 months; now my sales increased by nearly 35% and my payroll cost is still remaining the same. Amazing! I am making money. I need a planning session with Ying to work out a plan for the profit I am going to have this year. New problem ;) a happy one."

Dan's reply:

"She is a wicked witch [a reference to the Wicked Witch of the West in *The Wonderful Wizard of Oz*] of the business; remember? Your appointment is set tomorrow with Ying at 10am."

STARTING WITH GRANTS

Another possibility for starting a business is to get a grant from a nonprofit or from the city, county, or state government. This money could come to you non- interest bearing, but still it is not free, as Monahan said. What it will cost you is time and energy.

You will have to research the places where these kinds of grants are available, and you will have to invest the creativity and knowledge to complete the applications. Probably you will have to meet with a representative of one of these organizations in person, too. That is still a good deal to avoid the problems of a bank loan.

If you do get one of these grants, plan ahead how you will use it wisely. You must look ahead to the day when the money will be gone, and you will have to operate from your profits alone. Plan for how you will run the business on that day, when the grant money runs out.

As Barbara G. Berger, President of Food City Markets, Inc., has said: "The sun doesn't shine forever." While growth and expansion are always a priority, plans and preparation for major downturns and new competition can save a business in bad times."[41]

No money is free money, even if you get a grant to fund your project. Then you need to know how to qualify for the grant and how to continue to be qualified.

Non-Profit Help

You may be able to find grant programs, which will supply money that you do not have to pay back. In addition, there are many nonprofit organizations and local government-funded loan programs. These loans are underwritten differently than bank loans.

- They normally have more favorable interest rates or are interest free.
- They sometimes can loan to you even if you have a bad credit history.
- They normally do not ask for a personal guarantee.
- They do not have a loan fee like the bank would normally charge.

Some of my startup clients want to start a nonprofit organization because they think that government funds or donor funds can meet the operating needs. What they do not realize is how much compliance they need to meet in order for the first dollar to come into the organization.

And if you are willing to do the work to find a governmental agency or business helping nonprofit to help you with a grant or a loan, you will be much better off than a business owner who takes a loan from the bank.

Another good point about the business helping nonprofit is that they want to see your business succeed, partly because their mission and goal is to help small businesses to start up. So they may have resources like advisors or designated vendors.

As far as you as a business are concerned, regard the nonprofit you approach for help with a healthy respect. Do not assume that it has deep pockets and no needs. When you succeed, come up with ways to benefit this nonprofit that helped you.

GOVERNMENT HELP

Before you leave this chapter, I want you to know that many startups take advantage of government-offered programs. It is good for the government to help start new businesses. Then they are forming more taxpayers! That is good for everybody.

Here is where to look for federal government grants:

The Small Business Administration is a good source of help for new business: https://www.sba.gov/. It even has a special program for helping minority businesses.

You can also find information on the Department of Labor website that can help you find grants: https://www.dol.gov/general/grants/howto.

Grants.gov is the place to start when you want to find a federal government grant: https://www.grants.gov/

I have worked with the Iowa Economic Success Center before with my clients. The Immigrant Entrepreneur Summit that I founded has many resources to help people in Iowa and nearby states to start businesses. And you are always welcome to make an appointment with Community CPA to discuss funding for your business. We are happy to point our clients in the right direction!

Also, do not neglect the state, county, and city levels of government. At the state level, you will want to look up your state's department of commerce, department of labor, or department of human resources. The county should have similar departments, and it may be able to help with property tax relief. At the city level, you can find the official city website. Chances are, you will find official services or business liaisons devoted to promoting business.

Right here, right now, there is a huge divide between business owners who are seasoned in governmental assistance programs and business owners who are new to the USA. If you do not know, then you do not look. Now in this chapter, we say it loud and clear: there are many business-assistance programs that you can take advantage of if you just get on the Internet and research.

Business owners who are from the Country of the Head are the ones thinking through this path more naturally than those owners from the Countries of the Hand and the Heart.

FOOD STAMP PANIC

Speaking of government programs, different people view them differently. I saw one example of this truth in my client Samuel.

One day about nine months after we filed his income tax, Samuel showed up at my office and sat down in my yellow chair heavily. With a worried look, he said, "Ying, I think you guys did my tax wrong."

"Really? Why?" I asked.

"Well, after I submitted my tax to the resettlement agency, they told me that I am not going to have food stamps anymore." I understood his issue. I did not realize that he was on them. Of course he would be, as he was a newly settled refugee.

I wanted to say something, but he was in a hurry to explain: "I had food stamps before, and all of my folks have that. I am the only one do not qualify, and something must be wrong about my tax."

His breathing was labored, and he looked shocked. His big brown eyes were filled with fear.

Part of the Culture

Many refugees live their lives and raise their children in a specific social environment. Often they form new tribes and new groups, and as a group, the community and government offer them benefits to help them resettle and also help to preserve the culture. These good deeds have limitations. If the social group lacks successful entrepreneurs, then a lifestyle on food stamps could become normalized.

Even among business owners, the idea of being poor enough to need food stamps is not troubling or unusual. They are used to having very little. Often, what little they do have goes straight into the business.

It is very probable that Samuel did not know anybody who was not on food stamps.

When Samuel lost his food stamps due to his business income increase, he felt scared rather than accomplished. Because he had been living in a community using food stamps, he didn't know what to do without them.

GOOD NEWS

After five minutes of listening to him and searching his tax returns, I smiled. I sat him down and explained to him how well he was doing with his business last year. His adjusted gross income was high enough that he no longer qualified for food stamps.

"If your income is higher than the food stamp threshold, you would not get food stamps anymore. You paid taxes this year. Do you remember? You should be happy that you are making more money and you do not need the food stamps anymore." I tried to make a positive impression on losing food stamp qualification.

Samuel replied, "Really? But everyone else has it."

I shook his hand and congratulated him for disqualifying his family from government subsidized support. "You have done so well with your business that your family is no longer needing government help." When he looked perplexed, I added, "That is a good thing!"

"Are you saying food stamps is not for everyone?" he blurted out and looked at me surprised. "What do you mean? I do not have food stamps. It is for folks who do not have anything? Ying, everyone at my place has it. So it is not for immigrants?"

Yes, I knew what he meant. Being an immigrant is kind of special. I felt that way, too. But food stamps are not just for immigrants. In fact there were people who never, ever used food stamps to buy things.

I had used them before, but that was in China. Ever since I landed in North America, I have never, ever even looked into these welfare systems other than for my clients. These programs truly made these immigrants feel special and loved, but maybe Samuel could get a bit more education on how these programs were not meant for permanent enjoyment.

Finally, he left my office with a big, confident grin and a proud look on his face – proud of his own accomplishments and business success.

So income tax brought Samuel a shocker that he was not prepared to see. But a couple of weeks later, he came back and told me that he told this fact to his village folks, and they congratulated him. He was literally proud and went ahead telling me, "I am going to be like you, no welfare."

Samuel came back every year. Four years went by so quickly.

SUCCESS SPREADS

Recently, I saw him at Von Maur with shopping bags in both of his hands. He was doing his Christmas shopping. "Ying," he called.

"Samuel! How are you doing?"

With a big smile he said, "You mean my business? It is really good!" Then in a lower voice he added, "I need to come to see you because I think this year, I will pay a lot of taxes. I want to plan."

His voice was sweet and happy, and I heard no traces of fear or worry. He had become a confident businessman!

Now, as a successful business owner, Samuel has the power to return to his small community and share the possibilities and pride of doing well. Watching Samuel grow his business and helping him to celebrate milestones like outgrowing the economic need for food stamps and becoming a productive taxpayer is a rewarding experience for me. Working with him helps me to realize that with proper guidance and influence, folks will learn and will thrive.

BE LIKE SAMUEL

I tell you the story of Samuel because I admire him. He started with almost nothing. That is why he needed food stamps in the beginning for his family. As far as his business, he built his business without loans and without government assistance by saving what he could from what he made.

His business grew slowly and steadily. He did not take on a large expansion all at once. He had grown his business in such a way that his success surprised him.

This is what I would wish for any of my clients. I would wish them the determination and the discipline to survive with little until they could make much. I would wish them freedom from bank loans. I would wish them the kind of success and happiness that Samuel has now.

The principle of this whole chapter is to try to do your startup without a loan. If you take the time to plan and research, I know that you can do it.

THE LOST RING

We are coming to the end of planning how you can start or expand a business with loans or without them. Now I want to look a little deeper at the question of why you want to do so. I want to ask why you might be thinking about taking out a loan. For a question of that nature, I can think of no better help than

Eckhart Tolle.

In *A New Earth,* Tolle told the story of a friend of his who was dying of cancer. She had a valuable ring that had been passed down in her family. One day, this ring was missing.

Tolle's friend was distressed. She thought she knew who had taken the ring, and she wanted to know whether she should call the police or confront the suspect herself.

Instead of answering her worry, Tolle asked her a series of questions. "Do you realize that you will have to let go of the ring at some point, perhaps quite soon? How much more time do you need before you will be ready to let go of it? Will you become less when you let go of it? Has who you are become diminished by the loss?"

After some time for reflection, the woman was able to realize that her Being, her essence as a person, did not depend on having that ring. Whether lost or stolen, the ring did not subtract from who she was. And the act of letting it go could help her separate from her ego.[42]

I want you to take a calm and quiet moment to think about a loan. Think about all the reasons why you want to get this big lump of money all at once. Then answer this question: Will having this sudden amount of money add to who you are?

Will it?

Let us ask some other questions. Is it going to prove that you are a big deal? Is it going to keep your standard of living the same so that you don't have to sacrifice? Is it going to let you snap your fingers and have success now without waiting and saving?

Those last questions are ego questions. If you answered yes, then a loan will not be a good idea for you. We must always be careful in business that we are not asking money to do something it cannot do.

It can do ordinary things. It can buy materials. It can pay for help or space. It can multiply your hard work.

But it cannot do people things. It cannot make you feel important or satisfied or accomplished. It cannot take away your worry. It cannot guarantee your success.

It cannot change who you are.

REFLECTION #11: BEFORE GOING FOR A LOAN

In some cultures, borrowing money is morally unfit. My parents' generation would take pride in not borrowing and in spending only what they had. Times changed, and now people borrow. I have seen many going overboard.

	BEFORE GOING FOR A LOAN
1	*Make sure you are not going overboard.*
2	*What do you use the borrow money for?*
3	*If you are using the money to buy a machine, for example, so you can wrap dumplings faster, that is an example of, "Yes, you can borrow and buy the machine."*
4	*Do not forget: you did not get your money for free, and you have a $2,000 cost. In this example, we assumed you will sell all the dumplings that your machine is capable of making. What if your machine can only be used to 50% capacity? Then you will not make it if you run this calculation above.*

In the previous example, I assumed that not only can you pay interest to the bank ($2,000), but you also can pay the portion of the principal back to the bank as well. If you borrowed $25,000 for five-year-life equipment, the bank would want you to pay this principal back in three years before the machine loses all of its value. So you must have $8,333 a year cash flow to pay the bank back on top of the $2,000 in interest.

It is not cheap to borrow. It might work out a lot better to borrow from relatives and friends or to get into partnership.

THINK TWICE BEFORE YOU JUMP INTO LOANS.

	Do I Need a Loan?
1	*Make a pros and cons list. Use real numbers and details. This means that you will have to do your homework with the bank or the investor or program that you are considering. No money is free.*
2	*Compare your pros and your cons. What are they showing you about your desire for a loan? Is it a good idea?*
3	*Here is your assignment. Can you pursue the strategy instead of taking out a loan?*

REFLECTION #12: HOW DO YOU FEEL ABOUT MONEY?

Different business immigrants "feel" differently. The HEART feels in his emotions, the HAND feels in his physical energy (nerves), and the HEAD feels in his logic. When you answer the questions above, make sure that you are "feeling" from your gut center.

Recall what Eckhart Tolle asked about the loss of a thing: Does it diminish who you are? In light of that thought, consider what you feel about money, not what you think.

	Your Feelings about Money
1	*How do you feel about money?*
2	*How do you feel that it will change your life or your business?*
3	*Do you hope it will change who you are?*
4	*What physical sensations happen in your body when you consider money?*

Borrowed money is not a quick way to settle some of these sensations. Only borrow money when your need is identified clearly and emotions are not part of it. It is easier on the business immigrant from the Land of the Heart, as borrowing can simply mean more profit would come of it and that the calculation has already been done. The formula says: "I will make money." But for those from the Land of the Heart with a cultural background like myself, borrowing money is an action that I would ponder for a very long time. I have borrowed money, but I worked with someone from the Land of the Head to make that decision together.

CHAPTER 7

When Do I Hire My First Employee?

Startup business owners can easily forget that they are the first employee they should hire. It is true! You are your first employee. How you treat yourself determines the health of your company.

HIRE YOURSELF FIRST

I have seen many startup business owners come to me with unmatchable enthusiasm. Their whole being radiates the excitement of doing. Doing things they have always loved to do. Finally today, today is the day that life is going to be perfect here and after.

That is never the case! Entering a business venture is no different from working for your boss. The boss is no longer that bald-headed lawyer whom Emily can't run fast enough to stay away. The boss is even more unpredictable and mean. Let's call it Fate. Because you want to be in control of your boss, but heaven knows that you are not.

Imagine working on a job and working for your boss and not getting paid. You might say: "I am working for myself, and I do not care to get paid." Think again; is that really true? How long can you keep on putting out time and money and not getting any as return? How long can you keep working day and night not getting any sleep?

Your spirit will run low; your love for your business will deplete; your dream will turn to a nightmare. You, as a person, will be defeated to the core.

You need to pay yourself.

I do not mean just putting a reminder on your business journal. It needs to be a discipline. Know that you and your business are two different entities. You are not your business. In order for you to manage the business so that you charge the right pricing and cover your costs, you need pay yourself.

Of course paying yourself does not mean to starve your business from having more cash. Paying yourself means rewarding yourself with something valuable. Maybe taking a business training class in Las Vegas and treating yourself and the person who is behind the scenes supporting you. I do not need to do math here, but you know the majority of the cost for this training trip is deductible.

Give yourself something valuable like working flexible hours. Give a value and make that a payout for yourself being the business owner. Nowadays more and more companies offer owner-like benefits to the employees, like flexible hours, non-accountable reimbursement for car and home use, pension plans, and on top of all that, the extended paid time off.

Computer technology and the Internet have made jobs less and less dependable on location. Working at home and working whenever you like is much more common. So many jobs that used to be classified as an employee's job now are a contractor's job. This has created a new set of business owners.

LOST THE POSITION BUT NOT THE JOB

Will was an IT officer of a medium-size software company in Iowa. In 2008, the company got acquired by a California company. His position was eliminated. But he was offered a contract to continue to work for the next three years with total pay equaling to his gross salary.

The company required him to set up his own company, and contract payment would be paid not to him but to his company.

He came to see me. He could not believe that he was now a business owner, which was something he wanted to be but never knew how to start.

Will asked: "I listened to one of your seminars online, and I think I should go for an S corp. But I am not sure how to pay myself."

It is rare for a startup business owner to come to our first appointment and ask, "How do I pay myself?" The business owner from the Country of the Head does. They already have the outcome calculated, and they are not thinking about others at this point.

However, the business immigrant from the Countries of the Heart and the Hand are different. The business owners from the Country of the Heart are the most "forgetting-about-self" kind of people, and they will not think about paying themselves. Rather, they are already dreaming about paying a lot to their best employees.

"Do I need to pay myself a salary?" Stacie asked that question. She wanted to give every penny that she had to the poor.

Business owners from Country of the Hand do not think of paying anyone right away. Simply the product is the most important. If it sells, then naturally things and people will get paid. Paying themselves? The answer is always: it does not matter.

It is crucial to pay yourself. So business owners like Stacie can replace her broken car, drive around for more donated items, and serve more needy people.

It is necessary to pay yourself. So Will can continue to support his family with a paycheck from his own company.

It is discipline to pay yourself. So Samuel can stay away from the food stamps and not feel the cash flow pinch at his home.

THE SKI BUMP COUPLE

At 8am one day, I was running late for a young couple who were both employed at Wells Fargo. I knew them from my time working there. Both of them were well-established at the company and making six-digit salaries. With no kids, they had a lot of time to think of something to do.

They wanted to see me because the husband was planning to leave his full-time job and devote most of his time to house flipping. He had already done one house. It took almost six months to finish the home, but he netted $35k for six months of part-time work. That was not bad. He was encouraged to make many of these $35ks.

"I am happy for you," I told them. "What do you need from me?"

"Mostly advice," the wife said. "This business is a big change from a regular job. Is it really okay not to get paid for months at a time?"

"It is really okay for now," I assured her. "But you both are so used to the money you had from the full-time work for both of you, you have already had a spending habit that pleases you. You don't want to change that for very long."

They both liked to ski so much that they had earned the nickname of "the ski bump couple." They also like to ride Harleys around the town. All of these fun things are what I call their lifestyle.

They laughed. They knew that they could not live without their fun!

I added, "If the business endeavor cuts the fun things out, then for a year maybe, you are okay. You still are running on adrenaline for the new business. But it will not last long. Cutting down your fun spending is simply going to make you disappointed at what you do, and pretty soon you will be missing your 8 to 5 Wells Fargo job."

The Way to Last

I have seen clients completely losing interest in their businesses. Some have just trashed the business without even properly selling it. Do not let your emotion run your business. Step away from the excitement of starting or from the depression of failing so that you can think clearly.

You have to take care of yourself while working hard so you can last. You are the first employee you need to hire. Hiring an employee means that you are committed to pay wages or a salary.

Yes - you have to be committed to pay for yourself!

To plan a business without planning to pay yourself is very much like planning a trip without money. You feel the excitement of travel at first. Then you get somewhere and cannot eat or sleep comfortably. How are you going to enjoy the trip when you are miserable?

Do not short yourself. Your body can work hard without getting paid, but your mind will get you to quit your business if you do not take care of yourself. This is why you reward yourself with pay. If your mind is satisfied, your business will last.

You might say, "Well, what if I do not want to pay a salary to myself? I do not want to owe Social Security and Medicare on my pay yet. Could I do something else to reward myself?"

Yes, you can do that. Remember Jose? He cannot get a salary from his business. He gets dividends from the profits as a shareholder. There is always a way to manage expenses. But a reward to yourself must be one of those expenses.

To please yourself and be really satisfied with the progress of the new business, write down all the things that you feel are a benefit to you, and give each one a value.

OUTSIDE HIRES

After you hire yourself, watch your bank balance. Wait till you can pay a person fairly before hiring. I will show you later how to tell what pay grade you can afford to offer.

And when you do hire someone, look at the person as a whole, not just the resume. Someone who has good skills and education can be a miserable workmate. Consider the words and the spirit of the first employee carefully. They can bring happiness or stress to your business.

Richard "Bo" Dietl, Chairman of Beau Dietl & Associates advises, "Also, when hiring an executive assistant, I do not go with the candidate with the highest IQ; I go for the one who has the best all-around attitude. I prefer someone giving me 100 percent of what God gave them than someone with a high IQ giving me 50 percent. Having a good attitude makes for a successful relationship between the boss and the assistant."[43]

See how important that is about the attitude and the spirit? When your business is small, you only have one employee other than yourself. Then if this person is negative, 100% of your workforce is negative. If this person is positive, 100% of your workforce is positive. The smaller you are; the more important the first employee will be.

Hire with thoughts. Hire with purpose.

You can teach skills. You cannot teach kindness.

HUA HUA AND FEI

You will be very tempted to hire your family to fill the first roles in your company. Your family may love you so much that they will take less pay or work longer hours than another person. Be careful how you treat your family. Business is temporary, but family is forever.

Remember how Hua Hua's sister in law Fei was so powerful in

terms of influencing her husband? She was sure that her husband would follow her back to China if she left. The welfare of Hua Hua's business depended on the happiness of Hua Hua's sister-in-law.

Family members are key to your continuation of the business. You might think you'll be okay shorting yourself, but you cannot short others close to you. Treat them with consideration.

If you do not, you will create family dilemmas and fights. I have seen too many couples divorce over a business, whether failing or not. This is sad. Your business cannot matter more to you than your family.

Nail Shop Problem

One time a Vietnamese couple came to me with a problem. Viet, the wife, wanted to continue to work in the nail shop business, but the husband, Nam, wanted to close the company and be done with it. They made an appointment to ask me to decide for them whether to close or to continue.

Nam said, "She is so busy and works 12 hours day, and no time for the kids." He was mad! "I ended up helping her, too, at the store, and so no one is for kids."

"Who is taking care of the kids right now?" I asked.

Nam answered again. "Her mom stays at home and grandma does. But grandma does not even speak English and does not communicate with kids at all."

So we did a calculation.

"How much time would you like the kids to have with one of you?" I asked.

They consulted with each other and came up with a schedule: 5 hours a day from 4pm to 9pm.

My next question was: "How much money would you have to pay to get help at the store so mom can take off?"

Viet answered this time. "I will pay $20 for one hour." That

159

meant $100 for five hours.

"How much money would you like to pay to grandma since she watches over the kids?"

The grandma was watching the kids more for love and to support the couple than to earn money. But a token of kindness to her for her time would be $20 a day.

Being a mother myself, I did not want to forget the next question: "How much money do you have to pay for someone to cook your meals for your family each day?" Viet knew the answer to this question. They needed $40 for someone to cook dinner.

I added up the figures: $100 to employee; $20 to grandma; and $40 for dinner. "So you need $160 a day to be off work and be at home playing with the kids without doing housework. Do you think you can spare $160 a day?" I asked Viet.

She looked at me and said: "Of course." Nam nodded, too.

"Then it is done. With $160 a day budget to spend, this will allow you to be with your children regularly each day."

I always tell my clients that when frustrated with the situation in business, pull out a calculator. This answer is in the numbers.

A WAGE WORKSHOP

In my own practice in the early years, where my monthly income was at around $1,000, I knew what it would cost to run this small operation at home and to pay me about $50 an hour at the time. I knew my working hours on client's books.

My practice income meant that I had about $400 to use to hire someone else. If my work could be done by this person for a lesser hourly rate, I knew I could make it. Here is how I decided if I could hire someone.

For the $400 budget, if the hourly rate is $20 per hour, I can hire someone for 15 hours a month, not 20 hours. I have to remember to count the employer match to the payroll taxes, which adds to employer cost. The calculation is this:

*A. $400 * 75% / $20 = 15 hours.*

B. The 75% discount means that only $75% of the $400 is the real amount you can offer to your employee.

C. The 25% is a general amount for payroll budget, which includes the employer portion of Social Security and Medicare, as well as the state and federal unemployment insurance and workers comp insurance. I call saving this extra 25% off the top the "haircut rule."

All of my clients who hire employees know to obey the haircut rule when they are calculating how much in wages they can afford to pay. They know that the employee is getting more than what they take home. They get some benefit at some later time. The employee gets 25% more pay in the form of insurance, Social Security benefits, and Medicare.

If you apply the 25% haircut rule to the total money you have on hand to pay to employees, then the 75% is what you can pay employees. As long as you keep the payroll account under the 75%, then you know for sure that the amount of cashflow is sufficient for hiring.

Hiring the Best

When Donald Trump made his first significant deal after college to buy the subsidized housing development in Cincinnati, he needed a manager to collect rent, take care of the buildings, and manage workers. Trump hired a manager who was seedy and dishonest. He did not even keep regular office hours.

But this man, Irving, succeeded at the job. "Irving was the kind of guy who worked perhaps an hour a day and accomplished more in that hour than most managers did in twelve hours. I learned something from that: it's not how many hours you put in, it's what you get done while you're working."[44]

This is the answer of a Head person. Trump did not want to manage his manager. He wanted to trust that the man would get his job done, keep the money flowing, and not cause him problems. A Heart person would want to get to know him and help him improve himself, while a Hand person would object to the irregular hours and methods. Only a Head person could get along with an employee like Irving.

If Fred Trump was like his son, maybe he would hire men like Irving to help him in Brooklyn and Queens. However, Donald Trump focused his energies on Manhattan. There, he grew more demanding of his employees. Luxury property needed a luxury manager.

Trump searched very carefully for his manager for Trump Plaza Hotel and Casino, Stephen Hyde. "When I asked people in town to name the best casino executives, Hyde was always at the top of the list. As soon as we met, I understood why. He had a lot of gaming experience, he was a very sharp guy and highly competitive, but most of all, he had a sense of how to manage to the bottom line. A lot of managers focus on maximizing revenue since that's what gets reported publicly most often. The smarter guys understand that while big revenues are great, the real issue is the spread between the revenues and costs – because that's your profit."[45]

Stephen Hyde was working at another casino, but Trump was determined to hire him. "I have a very simple rule when it comes to management: hire the best people from your competitors, pay them more than they were earning, and give them bonuses and incentives based on their performance. That's how you build a first-class operation."[46]

Standards are very high at all Trump properties. Do you remember talking about Trump's brand? It is something that he can sell. His name on something means that it is first class – the best quality.

Here is a good bit of advice: "People will do what you measure and review."[47] In the Trump organization, there are standards people must meet to uphold the brand. These are objective standards that managers can measure and review.

Because Trump owns and runs so many properties in so many different places, he cannot oversee every detail at every property. He hires people he trusts to manage and hire employees who will honor the Trump brand. They all know that what they do reflects on that brand. So they know that no one who damages the brand will be retained, but those who reflect well on the brand will be promoted.

That is what we call a carrot and a stick. And using his name to provide the carrot and the stick works well for Donald Trump. "In my life, there are two things I've found I'm very good at: overcoming obstacles and motivating good people to do their best work."[48]

MANAGING EMPLOYEES

It is easy to do a math on the payroll amount you can afford. It is easy to take the haircut rule into account. The hardest matter for small business is to find that right person to hire. My first employee did not stay with me for very long, but my second employee who I hired was with my firm for 5 years. He was the person who taught me how difficult it is to manage one employee.

BUDGETING FOR STRESS

At the time, I was working at Wells Fargo. My title was Vice President of Controllers. I had managers, and those managers had employees. It was so natural to me that everyone respected my position and, so, respected me.

Wells Fargo was a well-established company, and the positions there were well defined. There was no issue about being a boss. My staff followed my directions without me needing to prove myself. My authority over operation was given.

When I prepared my departure from Wells Fargo to Community CPA, I had done many things to get ready. I saved enough money to invest in the Thomson Reuters system for the tax and accounting side of my practice. I budgeted left and right. I knew I could afford to pay rent and pay one employee.

But I did not budget the difficulty of managing just one person in your own business. I was completely taken by surprise. I could not manage one employee.

As a small business owner, you very seldom hire a person who will come with commitment and dedication. They work for you as the result of their life situation. It could work out, but in most of the cases, they do not last.

I learned that your employee's personal matters are important, especially if you have only a few employees. Do not tell them, "Don't bring your personal matters to work." In reality, to grow your employee and make that employee more committed to your business, you need to care about the employee's personal life.

You need to be able to put that person first.

Valuing Your Employees

Eckhart Tolle has told two stories that show an interesting relationship between two people. One is a king seeking advice from a wise man. The other is a pair of monks, one of whom has a more enlightened view than the other. When we listen to these stories, we can treat them in our minds like stories about an employer with an employee.

First, there was a king who was troubled by unstable moods. The things that happened in his kingdom would make him very happy or very sad. He could not tell from one day to the next how he would feel. These moods troubled him.

He heard about a wise man who was known for being at peace with himself and God. So he asked the wise man to come to him and help him. When the wise man arrived, the king explained his problem.

"Can you help me?" the king asked. "Can you show me how to find peace? I will pay you anything you want."

The wise man answered the king, "I can show you how to find peace. But the answer to your problem is so valuable that you cannot pay for it, even if you give me all your wealth. So I will give it to you freely if you will take it and use it."

The king promised that he would. The wise man left. Soon a box arrived for the king. Inside the box was a ring and a note. Words etched into the ring read: "This, too, will pass."

The king read the note from the wise man: "Wear this ring always. When anything happens, before you call it good or bad, touch the ring and read its message. That is the way to find peace."[49]

This knowledge that brought the king peace was exactly what he needed to hear. It was also something that was completely out of his power to invent or discover alone. He needed a wise person to help him.

If we look at the king as an employer and the wise man as an employee, we see that the king would have remained troubled if he had insisted that he knew all the answers and had instructed the wise man in how to advise him. We can see that sometimes employees are more gifted in certain ways than we are ourselves. We cannot let our pride stop us from benefiting from the excellence our employees bring to us.

Listen to this wise businessman: "Humility will guide you to use the things you don't know to your advantage. You will begin to seek out the brightest and best talent you can find without feeling threatened. You will begin to feel comfortable even if you aren't the smartest member of the management team. You will begin to hire people that compliment you by adopting this valuable philosophy: show me a person smarter than me, and I'll hire them."[50]

Here is the second story. Two monks, Tanzan and Ekido, were

walking along a muddy road in the country. They passed a village. On the other side, they saw a woman in fine clothing. She could not cross the road without ruining her clothes.

Tanzan saw the woman's distress. He immediately picked her up, carried her across the road, and set her down. The monks walked along in silence.

Miles later, Ekido spoke. "Why did you carry that woman across the road? You are not supposed to touch a woman so familiarly. You have broken your vows."

"I set her down miles ago," Tanzan answered. "Are you still carrying her?"[51]

I chose this story because it shows so simply a truth about employer and employee relations. There are handbooks and guidelines at many large businesses that detail how management and staff relate to one another. Within a large, corporate culture, maybe things need to be set down in black and white like that.

When you are running a small business, you must always take mercy into account. Yes, there are rules, and it is a good thing to have rules. But sometimes we must bend the rules in order to be kind to one another.

I think that this story is a good reminder for any employer that we are dealing with human beings with feelings and needs. Sometimes we are dealing with people in distress who need our help. Sometimes we are dealing with people who are discouraged, and they need a positive word.

These needs may not be spelled out in any employee handbook, but they matter. Your employees will remember much more how you made them feel than how strictly you kept an agreement. You will be much happier and run a much more successful business if you can regard your employees as a real asset to your company and not just a drain on your payroll.

JOINING A DREAM TEAM

Elon Musk has a unique relationship to his employees. He makes a lot of money, and he likes his toys. There is no question that Elon Musk has hired himself first. He also rewards his employees well, with good salaries and stock.

But working for Elon Musk is about much more than being paid well. Here is what you must know about hiring as far as Elon Musk goes. He does not really have to go out and find people. People come to find him. They want to do what he does. And they know that they can only do what he does if they work for him.

This situation affects the way Musk hires and manages his employees.

He works harder and for longer hours than anyone else at his companies. He is driven by his vision of saving the world through interplanetary travel and clean energy. So when he wants employees to work as long and as hard as he does, he can ask them. After all, he is not really asking for himself.

"It's the sweeping goal that forms a unifying principle over everything he does. Employees at all three companies are well aware of this and well aware that they're trying to achieve the impossible day in and day out. When Musk sets unrealistic goals, verbally abuses employees, and works them to the bone, it's understood to be – on some level – part of the Mars agenda. Some employees love him for this. Others loathe him but remain oddly loyal out of respect for his drive and mission…He's less a CEO chasing riches than a general marshalling troops to victory."[52]

Musk is a Hand person. So he is focused totally on the work he has to do. An employee at his company is an extension of Musk like his hand is an extension of his body. He expects this hand, this employee, to do what he would do if he were working in that area.

"Musk's demanding management style can only flourish because of the otherworldly – in a literal sense – aspirations of the company."[53] This inspiration and vision for the future motivates the employees more than Musk does personally. "Musk has taken industries like aerospace and automotive that the USA seemed to have given up on and recast them as something new and fantastic."[54]

Knowing how hard the work is, how tough the environment can be, and how long the hours are, you might wonder why anyone would want to work at SpaceX.But Musk has no shortage of applicants who can see his vision. "The recruiting pitch was SpaceX is special forces. If you want as hard as it gets, then great. If not, then you shouldn't come here."[55]

To work with Elon Musk is a privilege, and his employees all sense that.

So how does he hire them? When recruiting gifted engineers, Musk used tactics designed to arouse interest and make the candidate feel special. At conferences or seminars, only a handful of potential candidates would get unmarked envelopes containing invitations to apply. Candidates for all kinds of jobs had to pass rigorous tests, writing code on the spot, answering riddles, and completing an essay on why they wanted to work at SpaceX.[56]

One engineer, Bryan Gardner, met Musk at a party. The two hit it off, and Musk promised to get Gardner out of a prior contract. Gardner was hooked. "I emailed him my resume at two thirty A.M., and he replied back in thirty minutes addressing everything I put in there point by point. He said, 'When you interview, make sure you can talk concretely about what you do rather than use buzzwords.' It floored me that he would take the time to do this."[57]

Elon Musk has an intense work ethic. He also has an appealing dream. People know that when they ask to help him fulfill his dream, they must share his work ethic. They must become like little Musks, duplicates of him. They must become like his hands and feet, doing what he would do.

Because of this working relationship, Musk does not really have to hire. He gets to choose from the best. And the best will stay with him through any hardship as long as they share his dream.

Maybe you can do something like this in your small business. Maybe your company mission is so compelling or the products you make are so important that employees will seek you out. Maybe you will not have to be so careful about creating a kind culture if you are doing something so important.

But I think it is always better to be kind anyway.

Creating Goodwill

So I was involved with my one employee from renting an apartment to dropping him off to his apartment daily as he did not have a car. I did not see myself as a boss at all. I truly did not think it was an employer and employee relationship in our small business. It was in fact a brother and sister or mother and son kind of connection.

Don't listen to my story and then think that you have to hire your mother or your son! That would not work. But whomever you hire, treat that person like your mother or your son. That kindness will offer something that a large corporation does not offer. With time, this one employee you have will bring more to your workforce as you grow.

Being small is hard! You will lose your best employees because someone else is paying more. Look at the way Trump hires people that are good workers by offering lots of money! But I will just say that your best will come back if you are truly a good boss.

Life is not just about money. When you pay a reasonable pay, the rest of the benefits you offer personally then become emotional deposits. How much of an emotional deposit you make with your employees determines how well you can retain them.

I have loved every one of my employees. They left our firm for all kind of reasons, but they all became advocates for our firm. I made emotional deposits with them, but they did as well with me.

When you are ready to hire your first employee, yes, you should be sure to forecast your cash flow. At the same time, you must prepare your heart to love this person like you would love your child. Love this person that way even if the employee is older than you.

You may have heard something like the following advice: "Customer first, firm second, individual interests third."[58] Most times, you hear an employer saying this to an employee. When an employer says it to an employee, it means something like: "You don't matter. My business matters more than you do. If you are unhappy, you deal with it."

That does not make for a nice place to work. That does not make for a very conscious relationship between the employer and the employee. But I believe that there is a better way to take this good advice.

If the employer is the one who says this advice to himself or herself, then it means something different. As Mayo A. Shattuck III, Chairman, President, and CEO of Constellation Energy Group says, it means, "Other people are very valuable, and I want to treat them well. My business depends on treating them well! So I will give all the kindness and awareness I have to my customers and my employees. By loving them as people, I benefit my business. I will benefit myself by loving others."

An employer who can say that is building a business that is longlasting.

To be more specific, let's consider an example. You have a new accounting practice, like I did. Your only employee calls for the third day in a row saying, "I am still sick and coughing really bad." You hear that heartbreaking cough on the other end of the line.

You have an urgent job to finish, and you are waiting for your only employee to be back to help. You are waiting for the third day now, and you know your client is about to call and ask, "Did you get my project done yet?"

To test whether you are ready to hire an employee or not, tell me what you would do.

Do you hang up the phone and just said, "Okay, fine," while barely holding off your unhappy tone of voice? You think that your employee does not see your face and cannot tell your anger from your voice.

Wrong. You can forget about that. Your only employee was indeed sick, but he could come to work if he was motivated. Thanks to your unhappy tone, this reinforced his coughing and "I am sick, period." He was not motivated.

Put yourself in his place. Maybe he is having anxiety issues when he deals with the IRS. So his thoughts are making him sicker. Does an angry boss make things better for him? For you?

If you are really ready for having an employee, you will be warm on the phone. You will really be concerned about his health. You will ask if you could come by to bring something to him. You would do what mom would do for you when you are sick. You need to give up your right of judging.

Can you not judge your employee at all and be compassionate at all times?

Maybe now you are ready to hire your first employee.

REFLECTION #13: THE MAN-HOURS TEST

Let us consider the practical side of hiring an employee. How many man hours can your business afford? What additional costs do you need to consider?

THE MAN-HOURS TEST	
1	*First, complete the calculation that I did when I wanted to hire an employee. Write down how much money you have to spend on an employee. What number is that? Let's say that you have $1,000. Take 75% of that amount, and divide it by the hours that you need covered. $1,000 * 75%/40 hours=$18.75 per hour. That is what you can afford to pay.*
2	*You noticed that 25% of $1,000 is gone. We put it aside, and we are calling it a 25% haircut. Basically we are saying: "Don't think I am this tall, I am only 75% of the height, and my hair is 25% of the total height. The haircut rule – in business you always need to do this haircut before you calculate the hourly rate.*
3	*Use the calculation above to find the total cost of hiring your employee. Now you will use the kinds of questions I asked the nail shop owners to find the total cost of hiring someone. What daily life expenses should your business cover, like meals and childcare? What other expenses will you incur if you are not at your workplace: cleaning, customer service, delivery? Consider that your $1,000 of wages may need to cover more than one person doing more than one task. How can you split the amount per hour to be fair to all?*

REFLECTION #14: THE HUMAN COST TEST

Let us consider the human cost of hiring an employee. Ready?

THE HUMAN COST TEST	
1	*How does running your business make you feel? Are you happy, excited, stressed, sad? Be honest with yourself.*
2	*When you think of bringing another person into your business, how do you feel? Where do those sensations occur in your body?*
3	*What do you have to give an employee besides money? What benefit does the employee have from being around you regularly? Is working for you a good deal for that person?*

4	*What kind of person do those around you consider you to be? What do they say about you?*
5	*Do you have problems putting other people first? How does the idea of valuing other people above yourself make you feel?*
6	*How do you work with employees who are smarter than you?*
7	*If you are from the Land of the Heart, do you think you would get along with an employee who is from the Land of the Head? Would he be too smart for you?*

In my 10am book, I will talk about how to work with different employees. For now, ponder that question on your own, and share with me your thoughts.

Appointment with Ying @ 8am

CHAPTER 8

All the Taxes I Would Encounter in Business

A LESSON IN DISCIPLINE

Earl G. Graves, Sr. is the Chairman and CEO of Earl G. Graves Limited and Publisher of *Black Enterprise Magazine.* He has served as the chairman of the board of several important companies, including Pepsi, and he is very important in the world of media. He tells the story of learning about money as the grandchild of immigrants.

"The best business advice I ever received came from my father… a child of immigrants from Barbados who was orphaned in America at age fourteen…he taught me from a young age how to make money – and how to keep it. At fourteen, I landed my first salary job as a Western Union messenger. I made sixty-five cents an hour. Dad would take a cut for the household, put some away for my savings, and then give the rest of it to me. Without 'telling' me, he showed me that earning money was not the same as having it. If I was going to have money, I was going to need the discipline to save, the sense to invest, and the willpower to put my personal and material needs last."[59]

Earl Graves, Sr. learned the true principle at a very young age that not all the money that comes to us is ours to keep. What we owe, we must pay. If we pay it on time and do not avoid responsibility, we can keep from paying penalties and interest.

For an immigrant like myself, the word "tax" carries a negative tone. I was taught in middle school in China that tax is a byproduct of capitalism and a tool for the government to enrich themselves and rob the poor. A lot of people who are not from Western countries think of tax that way, too!

Working with startup entrepreneurs, there are times I recognize the defensiveness of the immigrant business owners who are obligated to pay taxes from the company's profits. The bad feeling is almost not about paying taxes. It is more the feeling of being robbed.

One immigrant who can show you his story of learning about taxes and regulations is Phillip.

PHILLIP: A CASE STUDY IN BUSINESS TAXES

Phillip, who is an immigrant from Sudan, talked to me about taxes back home. Phillip's family operated a farm in Sudan. A government official came and took everything and left the family a note saying: "You owe taxes." Where he comes from, in that war-torn country, the government just "came and took, no questions asked, and they just came and took."

PHILLIP'S IMMIGRATION

Now Phillip lives in a place in Iowa where other Sudanese are there as well. The place has many familiar faces to him, and they all come from the same refugee camp. They choose to come to Iowa out of all the state choices they could have made.

If you ask Phillip why he came to Iowa, he will say, "I want to see a lot of land and crops and open spaces. So the immigration officer told me: then go to Iowa. That is why I came here." The sense of space and peace here was very much like his hometown before the war. He also told me that he felt very special here and people care about him.

Phillip has this very large smile and dark, dark skin that is shining and smooth, white teeth and dimples on both cheeks. Very gregarious looking young man. He is a person that other people like.

PHILLIP'S RESTAURANT

Phillip started a small Sudanese fusion restaurant. When he first started operation, we explained to him about payroll taxes because he had one cook. Based on the 25% haircut rule, we told him that if he planned to pay the cook a $10 an hour rate, the real cost to him for this cook without overtime was $12.50 per hour.

Recall that the total payroll cost is not just what the cook took home, it should also have Social Security and Medicare match, worker's comp, and unemployment insurance with the federal and state governments. If a business can afford to pay for $10.00 an hour based on cash in the bank, offer the employee $7.75 an hour where it is legal, because you have other costs coming.

Phillip was well prepared for the payroll taxes. He also was well prepared for sales tax, as we told him that this is the money you collect for the government and you pay to the government as an agent or the trustee who handles the collection. It was not your money from your business. That was really clear to him, too, and he managed this payment timely.

But use tax was somewhat a hard concept to him, and he did not get it. In the end, he said: "I will just not buy things online. Or at the end of year I tell you what I bought online, and you can check my invoices to make sure I paid use tax."

State unemployment insurance was also like a tax that you had to pay as long as you have employees. Workers comp came in like taxes, too. Phillip was surprised that he had to pay them. But at least the 25% haircut rule covered the cost, and so he was somewhat prepared.

PHILLIP'S LANDLORD

Phillip's landlord stopped at my office. "May I see Ying, please, just for five minutes." I came out. He did not have an appointment with me. Luckily, I was around.

"I just had an argument with my new tenant Phillip this morning, and I was trying to tell him that other than rent, he also needs to pay a CAM fee. He was telling me that the CAM fee is too high; he does not like it. I was trying to explain to him that the property tax is included in the CAM fee. Phillip said he knew all the taxes and there is no such thing about property tax."

I could not help smiling, because I knew why Phillip was telling him that. The other day when Phillip was here, he asked about buying property. I told him that once he knew which property he wanted to buy, we could calculate a rent roll for him to determine if he could have enough cash flow to pay the property tax and be a landlord. The way I said it, he understood that property tax belongs to people who own a property.

I promised the landlord I would explain things to Phillip. Before the landlord left, he asked: "Do you speak Sudanese?"

I replied quickly: "No."

"Then why is it he can understand you but not me?" he asked.

I just smiled. Some things, you cannot explain.

PHILLIP'S INCOME

Phillip came in right after the new year. He said, "Someone from your office called and said I need to file income tax."

I welcomed him for coming to file his first ever business tax return with us. I looked at the income and loss statement that he prepared. He was doing so well! On the very bottom, he had $25,000 net profit for the year.

For the first year, he received a targeted small business loan from Iowa Economic Development Authority for $50,000 with only a 3% interest rate. So his interest expense was only $1,500. He used all of those funds to purchase the equipment in the restaurant. Imagine the depreciation deduction that he would get, which would offset all of his profit!

His restaurant was an S corporation. His restaurant profit would go to his personal return to be taxed.

Phillip asked: "So for $25,000 profit, how much income tax would it be?"

I looked at the purchase price of the equipment and calculated depreciation. Then I said: "Literally 0."

"What? Income tax is zero; are you sure?" his white teeth and dimples were just so pleasing to see.

I explained the value of his depreciation. He smiled more.

HELPING CHARLES

Phillip learned that when he started to do business in the USA, he encountered the following taxes right away:

1. *Payroll tax*
2. *Sales tax and use tax*
3. *Unemployment insurance (acts like tax)*
4. *Workers comp (acts like tax)*
5. *Income tax*
6. *Property tax (through the landlord's CAM fee)*

For Phillip's business, he also had to renew his food license for the business. He did not sell liquor in the restaurant. Otherwise he would need to apply for a liquor license.

His company was an Iowa corporation with the Iowa Secretary

of State. So there was a biennial renewal that needed to be done for the business.

All of these taxes, licenses, and fees were things Phillip learned. Phillip felt pretty confident that he knew the ropes now, and he was eager to help. One of the fellows in his village, Charles, approached him to set up a tax preparation service. So Phillip explained to Charles all the steps to get the business started.

The tax store started, and Charles came and visited me once prior to his opening. From Phillip, he learned to set up payroll tax accounts. A professional service in Iowa had no sales tax, and so he knew not to charge sales tax but registered use tax. He also planned on unemployment insurance and workers comp.

Things for his business were really complete, except he did not take a training class for professional tax preparers, as it was not mandatory in Iowa. He did not pay income taxes. Instead, he always got a refund as he had 5 children ranged 2 months old to 8 years old.

Different businesses had different requirements on taxes and license requirements. Phillip helped Charles a lot. But because Charles had a tax business, not a restaurant, Phillip could not know all of the regulations and licenses that would apply to Charles.

REGULATIONS AND LICENSES

Seth Waugh, CEO of Deutsche Bank America says: "Clients have often told me that they want two fundamental things from a relationship: Trust and Consistency. Any decision that destroys the first or undermines the second may be a decision you spend your life trying to get beyond."[60]

I can tell you that this is what the government wants from you, too. It does not matter if it is the small city government where you live or the big IRS. The government wants to trust that you are who you say you are and that you do what you say you will do.

They want things to line up neatly.

If one business submits a form saying, "Hey, I hired this business over here to do catering at this time, and I paid them this much money," then they want to see a line on the catering company's tax form saying, "Yes, I got paid this much money from this business on this date." They want all the numbers to match. When the numbers do not match, they start asking questions.

There is another part to what the government watches. It is their job to make sure that all citizens are safe and that no one can hurt other people. That is why they license and regulate businesses.

Before regulation, businesses could dump chemicals into streams and on land. That would poison drinking water, making fish and wildlife die and making people sick. The government stepped in and said, "You cannot do that anymore. The land and water belong to all of us. You cannot make us all sick so that you can make money."

It is the same with other regulations and licenses. Because there are licenses, you know that the person who cuts your hair has had training. You know that the place that serves you tacos or spaghetti is clean. You know that the bank where you keep your savings will not close tomorrow and take your money.

You have this safety as a buyer. Now it is your privilege to give this safety to your customers.

Donald Trump

Licensing and regulation affect every business owner, not just small business owners. Sometimes it seems like people with a lot of money can do whatever they want to do. But that is not true. They have to obey government rules, too.

Remember the conversation that Donald Trump had with Victor Palmieri about the bankrupt railroad property? Palmieri liked Trump. He got him started on the Commodore Hotel, which the railroad also owned and needed to sell.

Around the same time, in 1974, Donald Trump optioned the railroad lands for $10 million. If he could have built anything that he wanted on that land, then he would have sold the apartments and rented the office space and shop space. He would have made a lot of money and moved on to the next project.

But he could not do that. He had to listen to community boards, architecture critics, and city planners. These people said that the buildings Trump wanted there would block their windows, put too much traffic on the streets and subways, and cost the government too much money.

Trump tried so many things to please these boards and planners. He fired the architect he liked and hired another one that other people liked. He promised public parks. He met with city officials. Nothing worked.

In the meantime, the land that should have been making him money just sat there. Trump still had to pay the bank a mortgage for the land. He had not expected to pay a mortgage on a land that was not earning him money. Finally, he had to sell his option to a group of Chinese investors in 1994.[61]

That had to be a bitter defeat. He had waited and planned and worked and lost money for twenty years. Then he had to give up.

Don't feel too sorry for Donald Trump! He had other projects to bring him money. I tell you this story to show you that you are not the only one to change plans and pay penalties because a city or a state government tells you what you can and cannot do. That kind of thing happens to everybody.

SMALL BANKING

One time an Asian lady named Lana came to my office and told me, "I need your help to set up a bank, and could you help me? I already have one, and I just need to make it official."

After talking to her, I understood. Lana was loaning small amounts of money to her community members, and the return of interest was like 500% annually. For example, she would loan $500 on Monday, and by Friday she will get $550 back or $50 back for interest. So in one year (52 weeks) she would make over $2,500 in interest.

Lana said: "I am making good money, but I know I do not have any taxes to pay till the end of year. That is why I did not come to see you yet. But I want to set it up properly so I can do more."

She is right. She does not have sales tax to pay on interest. She also does not have payroll, as she is on her own and operating as sole proprietor at this time.

But Lana does not have the license to operate what she is doing right now. In Iowa, if she loans to clients regularly, e.g., more than 25 clients in a year, she will be in violation of banking regulations in Iowa. To be legal, Lana has to stay very small.

Understand what the requirement of your line of business is, and consult with Community CPA. That is the best first step you take. If you are not close to a Community CPA branch, then find an attorney or accountant close to you.

Ultimately, Lana did not get her bank established. But knowing how the consumer lending works in Iowa, she continued doing the small loans and stayed on a very small scale. That way, she would not be in violation of the consumer lending act.

Several years later, I saw Lana again. She told me that she decided not to do the small loan lending anymore, as she lost all her capital. Her clients were concentrated on a number of workers from one factory that went bankrupt, and her clients all stopped paying.

Elon Musk

Elon Musk is another example of how everybody has to obey regulations. You may be thinking about my small banking client and saying to yourself, "That is actually a pretty good idea! Maybe I should open a bank and earn $50 a week!"

You, too, will run into licensing issues and many regulations telling you how you can run your small bank. The government wants to make sure that all money is safe. It does not want another Black Friday like in the Great Depression to happen. It wants people to trust banks and save up their money.

When Elon Musk first started X.com, which would later merge with PayPal, he was no stranger to the banking industry. In college, he had worked for a Canadian bank as an intern. He had seen portfolios of third-world debt.

All of this debt was insured by the United States government. If these poor countries defaulted, the United States said that it would pay. Musk told his boss that he should buy as much as he could. In his mind, the bank could not lose money unless the entire United States government collapsed. That was not going to happen!

But his boss wouldn't hear of it. That idea was outside what the bank traditionally did. Musk was frustrated at what he saw as an opportunity lost.[62]

When Musk started X.com, he wanted to seize the kinds of opportunities banks were letting slide by. He put in $12 million of his own money and got to work. He faced a large learning curve about money and finance, despite his earlier bank experience. So he hired talented bankers as well as gifted software developers.

In order to proceed legally, Elon Musk went to the authorities. "The company secured a banking license and a mutual fund license and formed a partnership with Barclays."[64] The Barclays website says, "Barclays traces its ancestry back to two goldsmith bankers, John Freame and Thomas Gould, who were doing business in Lombard Street, London in 1690. In 1736, Freame's son, Joseph took his brother-in-law, James Barclay on as a partner, and the name has remained a constant presence in the business ever since."[65]

He may have been starting a banking revolution with X.com. But Elon Musk could not have gone to anyone more reputable than that! And to get a license, Elon Musk had to apply to the state and survive many rounds of applications and background checks.[66]

He could not just say, "I'm rich, and I want to start a bank with my own $12 million."

Neither can you. Whatever kind of business you want to start, you have to find out the rules and regulations. For a restaurant, you need a license. You need to be inspected to make sure that your place is clean and your food is safe. For a school, you need to register with your state's department of education and have your students take standardized tests. Every kind of business needs some kind of permission.

THE FIFTEEN-YEAR MISTAKE

I know one heartbreaking story of how ignorance of regulations can ruin your dreams.

Hector was one of my very dear clients. He worked at a car repair shop and was a well-known car mechanic in our area. He dreamed for years to have his own auto repair shop with his name on a street sign in the front. A hard worker and good planner, he saved regularly. Over fifteen years, he finally saved $20,000.

When a piece of property came up for sale that looked ideal to him, he bought it, paying a lower price than he had expected. He was excited at his good deal. Finally, his dream of a car repair shop would come true!

Hector came through our front desk with music on his feet. He was beaming with joy. I was so happy to see him finally ready to open his own repair shop, especially after learning his workplace was going to close in a couple of months. What a good timing, too!

But it was not to be. After the purchase, he discovered that his new property was not zoned for a car repair shop, even though next to the property was a gas station. He could not run a business on that property he had bought.

He was stuck with a piece of property that was useless to him. Saving another $20,000 would delay his dream by another fifteen years at minimum. Especially now he would not have that job anymore in a couple of months' time.

The lesson that Hector learned is to look before you leap. Find out the regulations like zoning that you will encounter before running into them. Don't make mistakes like that which will delay your American Dream.

HONESTY EQUALS FEARLESSNESS

I like this quote from Henry R. Silverman, Chairman, President, and CEO of Cendant Corporation: "Our system of capitalism is built on the presumption of honesty, respect for the rule of law, and the assumption that institutions of stature and credibility will tell the truth…We have an unwavering obligation to tell the truth, tell it all, and tell it now to shareholders, employees, and customers who have placed their trust in our companies."[67]

The reason I like this quote is that it puts all businesses on the same level. We all have this duty to be truthful to our customers, to our employees, to our governments, and to ourselves. Mr. Silverman says that all of capitalism rests on this one virtue: honesty.

I can say from my own experience and from the experience of my clients that honesty does more than promote capitalism. It also brings peace. People who follow the rules and who know that they are following the rules never have a reason to worry.

They never have a stab of fear when an inspector walks through the door. Their hearts do not race when they see an envelope from the government. April 15 holds no terror for them. They are happy to do good work, and they sleep well at night.

That kind of feeling is priceless.

Fear of Authorities

But fear of authorities is a normal life experience for new immigrants and immigrant business owners. They have a lot of reasons to be fearful. Many immigrants come to the United States through United Nations immigration programs. They survive oppression and danger in their home countries, living in refugee camps for years until finally being chosen to resettle in the United States.

They fear that the Citizenship and Immigration Service could steal their American dreams and make them abandon their friends and families. They know that the process of applying for the Green Card and getting it into their hands could easily occupy another 10 years of their life. And at any time, for reasons they might not understand, it could be taken away.

So when Department of Labor auditors unexpectedly show up at an immigrant-owned business work site, they mean nothing but fear to the immigrant. The visit may be just a routine or caring gesture from the DOL. But for the immigrant, his mind is hijacked by his fear.

When immigrant taxpayers get an audit notice from the IRS, some may not seek professional help. Instead, they may abandon their apartment and move, leaving behind the growing pile of IRS letters. This fear breaks my heart, because I know that a little knowledge could save these people trouble and loss.

Business immigrants can experience this kind of fear, too. You do not have to fear deportation or the authorities. The solution is the same for everyone, whether you are just a business immigrant or also an immigrant coming to the USA.

Knowledge and Hope

The fearful minds of immigrants need a lot of education and care. So professionals must help immigrants address their issues with various government agencies, particularly when new immigrants are in business. Experienced Americans need to educate them and provide a road map to show them how to do things correctly from the beginning.

I met an immigrant who had been in business for almost 10 years without knowing he should be submitting sales tax regularly. He was so fearful that he did not seek professional help until his wife contacted me. She explained to me that her husband was terrified about their tax situation and was afraid of going to jail. So they were planning to move out of the U.S.

They did not have to move out of the U.S.! Their fear arose from their lack of knowledge regarding state and local taxes. With some guidance, they set up an installment plan with the state in less than two weeks. They could not believe how easy it was to correct their mistakes.

I remain open-minded when working with immigrants. I do not jump to conclusions, and I do not rush to believe that they are hiding something. When they tell me their problems, I stop and praise them for being honest in business dealings. I know that most of them are good people who are just misguided by fear. For them, overcoming fear is the first step toward their American Dream.

Eckhart Tolle

The important point about fearing the authorities is that fear comes from a lack of knowledge. When the mind lacks knowledge, it will make up stories about the unknown. These stories always cause worry. They also keep you from finding out the truth.

When you know the truth, you can live in the truth. You can do the simple, ordinary things that other people do to comply with the authorities. Do you really think everybody with a business has some special magic power to keep them from being audited, fined, or shut down? No. They all comply with simple rules. You can do that, too.

Eckhart Tolle tells a beautiful story about connection with the earth against the workings of the mind. Once, a monk and his disciple were walking in the mountains. They sat down to eat lunch under a tree. When they were done, the disciple asked a question.

"Master, how do I enter Zen?"

The master did not answer. The silence grew. In the silence, the disciple's mind worried about the answer to his question. He worried about whether his master would answer him or what the answer would be.

Finally, the master spoke. "Do you hear that little stream?"

"No, I don't!" the disciple answered. Was this stream part of the answer? Had he missed something important?

When the master did not speak again, the disciple grew quiet. He listened and listened to the world around him. Finally, in the silence, he did hear the quiet sound of a stream flowing over rocks.

"I hear it!" the disciple exclaimed.

"Enter Zen from there,"[68] the master instructed.

Can you see how the disciple's mind kept him from knowing peace? He was so worried about learning a secret or being good enough that he could not relax and connect to the world around him. He needed to grasp something real before he could find peace.

This is true for you. You cannot will yourself to get rid of your fear of the authorities. You cannot just make up your mind, "I am not going to worry anymore." This is not how minds work.

You need to feed your mind true facts about what you are expected to do. Then you need to come up with a plan to do what the authorities want you to do. It is not hard. And you can always find a CPA or a lawyer, like a business Zen master, to show you the realities that will ease your fears.

The story of the monk and the disciple does not end with that moment of insight. The two men kept walking through the mountains, and the disciple at first remained amazed at the aliveness of the world. Then he began to worry again about the answer to his first question.

"Master, what if I had not been able to hear the mountain stream? What would you have said to me then?"

The Master stopped and looked at his disciple. "Enter Zen from there."

This is a beautiful story. Whatever your situation, no matter how many IRS letters you have stuffed into the back of a drawer, there is always a way forward. You can always turn toward knowledge and peace, no matter where you are.

It is never too late to do the right thing.

REFLECTION #15: PLAN TAX PAYMENTS

In business, planning can lead to peace and prosperity. Then we must know what to plan, right? So here we are going to test what you know about your business' critical planning areas.

Taxes are so important. Depending on your tax structure, you will pay taxes at different rates and different times of the year. What is your tax structure? When is your tax due? If you have employees, do you plan for the haircut rule to make sure you have all of the necessary taxes and insurance paid?

Look at this list of the kinds of taxes Phillip paid. Do you have enough cash flow to pay all of these taxes? If you honestly do not even know, then you need to call Community CPA to help you! To have peace you must plan.

PLANNING TAX PAYMENTS	
1	*Payroll Tax*
2	*Sales tax and use tax*
3	*Unemployment insurance (acts like tax)*
4	*Worker's comp (acts like tax)*
5	*Income tax*
6	*Property tax (perhaps through a landlord's fee)*

REFLECTION #16: LICENSES & REGULATIONS

Now let's talk about licenses and regulations. No matter what kind of business you have, your city, state, county, and the federal government will have something to say about how you run that business.

LICENSES & REGULATIONS	
1	*Start small with your city government. Look up the licensing and regulation for operating your kind of business in your city. Maybe you will have to talk to your city Chamber of Commerce. What kind of rules apply to you? Have you done everything you can to operate legally?*
2	*Move one step up to the county government. Counties can regulate things like property taxes, zoning, schools, and alcohol sales. What county regulations and licenses apply to your business?*
3	*Now look at the state government. How does the government of your state regulate or license your business in your state? Look up the laws that apply to you. You can do some research by talking to other business owners in your state that do the same kind of work you do. How do they stay in compliance with the state?*

Appointment with Ying @ 8am

CHAPTER 9

Meet with Ying

GETTING STARTED

Appointments are a way of life at Community CPA.

Jose is someone I truly admire. As my client for the past 20 years, I have seen him truly realize his American Dream through unbelievable hurdles. As he always said during those difficult times, "I am happy even just to breathe the air of the USA."

Over the years, Jose has gone through situations that are seemingly unique to him. I thought if I simply added up the communication between Jose and my firm, then I could provide readers with a glimpse of one of our challenges in the real small business startup world.

MEETING JOSE

Jose learned about me from one of his friends. His friend told him, "There is a lady names Jing." (Many of my Spanish-speaking clients call me Jing, and that is okay with me!) "She does not speak Spanish, but somehow you will understand the way she talks, and she will understand you, too."

Somehow that was our firm's reputation from the get-go. We

later on started to hire folks who speak other languages. As of today, we have more than 20 employees, and every one of us at the firm speaks another language. We are a professional services firm that is committed to speaking our clients' languages.

Jose first came to my office in the summer of 1998.

He came to us speaking broken English, but he was pretty good at speaking it. For me, I know just a few words in Spanish. I was grateful that he spoke English.

"Jing, I did not have paper. But I have a small business, and I need your help. I do not know how to pay taxes. I want to do everything correct with my business and my personal tax. Could your company help someone like me?"

I understood what "no paper" means. Later on, Jose told me his story of coming to the country via freight train – literally shipped over like a piece of lumber. He has always been so proud of the fact that he paid the agent back all the money he owed in 6 months' time.

SOME PAPERS

To do everything correctly, we must have some kind of ID. So I asked, "Do you have any ID?"

"No, I do not have any ID. But my name is real."

That was not good enough for establishing a tax ID in the USA. So I recommended him to go to the Mexican Consulate in Omaha, Nebraska to obtain a consular card for himself and use that as an ID. Jose went the following week and came back to me with his brand-new consular ID – Jose Luis Hernandez.

With his consular card, we started the process of applying for an Individual Taxpayer Identification Number with the IRS. Jose may not have had an American social security card, but he was going to pay all the American taxes like any other taxpayer. In about three-months' time, we received the ITIN for Jose.

Jose was so excited. When he arrived at the office, he extended his arms to give me a hug. It was so touching to see him so appreciative of what we had done so far. He also told me that some states would even allow him to get a driver's license with the consular card and ITIN.

ELON THE IMMIGRANT

Elon Musk wanted to come to the USA early in his life. He told one PBS interviewer, "And you know I wasn't born in America -- I got here as fast as I could."[69]

Elon's father Errol was from South Africa. His family had been there for hundreds of years. Elon's family on his mother's side had lived in the USA and then Canada before coming to South Africa, where he was born and raised. The Haldeman family originally were Swiss Germans who came to the USA during the Revolutionary War and traveled west.

A branch of the Haldeman family moved to Saskatchewan in 1907. They were chiropractors, although Elon's grandfather Joshua did many other jobs, including breaking horses and organizing rodeos. Joshua Haldeman was also an amateur aviator who flew around the world with his wife, Wyn.

Partly in frustration with the Canadian government and partly in search of adventure, Joshua and Wyn Haldeman emigrated to South Africa with their five children.[70]

Maye Musk, Elon's mother, married a native South African. But her Canadian birth certificate meant that Elon had an easy time moving to Canada at the age of 17. And from Canada, passage to the United States was only a student visa away.[71]

It is fortunate for the USA that doors opened so easily to allow Elon Musk to become an immigrant. The USA benefits from Elon Musk's energy, creativity, and intelligence.

Can I tell you a secret? Jose Hernandez also has energy, creativity, and intelligence. And no matter how he came to this country, we are lucky to have him. Jose is a good person and a gifted immigrant to the Land of Business – just like Elon Musk.

Legal Business

I explained to Jose that the type of corporation that our lawyer established for him was called a C corporation. The company would run as if this corporation was an individual with the proper status to work in the USA. It would track its own income and expenses, and it would pay taxes under the company name.

"Since you don't have working status or paper, you cannot get business licenses or permits and cannot go out to bid jobs properly. You may not even be able to buy liability insurance. But your company is like a US person, and you can do all that under your company. You can also pay yourself dividend income from your company to help support your family."

Jose said, "I will make a lot of money, and I do not mind at all to pay taxes. I just want to do it right."

DBA:
Doing Business As

Jose needed to give a name to his new corporation, and that took a little long to decide. Prior to forming the company, Jose asked one day: "I was doing these jobs under Hernandez Fix. If I want a different name, what is going to happen to Hernandez Fix? What if I still get paid under Hernandez Fix?"

"That is not an issue," I told him. "We can put all the names you used like this one- Hernandez Fix - to be a DBA name, Doing Business As. So if a client writes a check to your new corporation, then you would still be able to deposit it to your business account."

"Really? That is great! Can you also put in 'Jose Repair'? I used this one, too, and I still have some folks write me checks under this name."

"Do you have time to come in and meet with the attorney?" I asked. "He will help you to get this all done. Please think about a name or two for the corporation."

"Okay. Do two DBA names, and for my new corporation, I want the initials of my son to be the name of the machine shop. Can I call it DDH Machinery Company?"

"Of course, that's okay, unless someone else in Iowa is already using that name. That is why you need to think of another one in case this one is not available."

"Jing, you are the best, and done deal. Please get it set up the right way."

Jose opened a bank account for his new company, and business was going really well. The only way I knew it was going well was that I was checking on direct deposit payroll third party fee each month. I saw DDH on it all the time. That meant they were doing well and staying active.

EXPANDING THE BUSINESS

HIRING EMPLOYEES

Jose emailed me in Sept 2010:

"Jing, do you have time to talk about hiring employees? You told me that I cannot be an employee of other employers because I have no paper, but can I hire employees? I want to hire a mechanic. I need help. Please let me know what I would need to give you so you can run payroll for my employees."

My reply: "Jose, it would be just fine to hire employees. For every employee you want to hire, please provide us the following. I have attached the forms for you, and so you can just print them out and give them to the person who is going to work in your shop. Do not have them work there yet till these forms are done:

- I–9: This must be filled out prior to hire; please sign as employer, too, in the section that I highlighted for you.

- W-4: This is for withholding. In case your employee does not need you to withhold income tax, this form will tell us.

To set up the payroll service for your company, please provide me with your payroll account routing number and account number. I will run the payment to the IRS and state from this account. Do you remember the 25% haircut rule on payroll? Do not over hire, and be gentle to your cash flow."

The Subcontractor

Jose called the next day to discuss our emails.

"Jing, I just found out that the person I like to hire, he works at another place as subcontractor currently doing something like what I want him to do. So he wants to work with me on demand, whenever I need him. Thus he wants to be paid as 1099 contractor. Is this OK? Can he be a contractor instead of an employee?"

I explained to Jose the difference between subcontractors and employees. In his field, most mechanics were employees. However, in this particular situation, one could effectively argue that the person was working on the same kind of skills as subcontractors for multiple clients. I thought it was worth exploring why this person was not an employee with the other company.

"Did you say he was doing the same thing with another company on demand? How do you pay him if he is on demand?" I asked.

"I will pay him by hours," Jose said.

"That sounds to me like an employee. Is there a way to find out how he was paid by the other company? Maybe they are paying him by jobs. Then it is best practice to pay him by jobs, not by hours, if you were going to treat him as subcontractor."

Jose got back to me a couple of days later and told me that the other company was paying this person by time. But he also added: "They just recently changed him to be an employee. That is why he is looking to be a subcontractor elsewhere."

So I explained to Jose that the company realized that they were doing it wrong; so they made changes. Of course, that change brought down the net pay to this person. So he was looking for a place where his net pay would equal his gross pay. It might not have been a contractor vs. an employee issue. It was a skilled worker who wanted to be paid more.

Jose ended up hiring him as employee but paid his net pay to equal the gross pay that he got from his prior job. Jose did everything legally, and both parties were happy.

The Injury

Jose texted me. One of his employees injured his hand while working. The employee was rushed to the hospital. Jose had been waiting in the emergency room with the employee for a couple of hours already and had just now had a chance to text me.

"SOS Guy is injured bad."

I looked at the message and then checked the payroll records on file. Then I texted back: "He is okay and covered by insurance; I will file a worker's comp claim. Hospital will ask you and just provide the info."

"Okay."

"The 25% haircut includes the cost of this insurance, and you are just fine."

"What if he sues me? Everybody sues in USA."

"The workers comp insurance will take care of that, and your general liability insurance may also cover some. Make sure you always pay your premiums on time."

199

The Claim

Jose texted me one morning urgently.

"Jing, someone is in my office and wants my tax ID. Which one is my tax ID? ITIN or EIN? Help."

I replied, "Put me on the phone with this person."

The phone rang and the person with Jose started to talk. "Hi, my name is Travis from ABC Insurance Company, and I am here to collect some information regarding that worker's comp claim so that I can complete the case file. I need the company tax ID."

"Okay, sure. I will email that to you." I replied. I got his information and hung up.

Then I texted Jose: "I will give the company ID to him. Everything related to your business, when people ask for an ID and come to your business location, goes under your company EIN number, not your ITIN number."

"Yes, Jing! Thank you. But when would they ask me for my tax ID?"

"No one should ask for your personal tax ID unless you are being audited."

Thinking Big

I read an article recently that listed five success tips from Donald Trump. I thought that these ideas were very good, and I wanted to share them with you. Part of the reason I want to share them with you is that they remind me not only of Donald Trump, but also of Jose.

5 Success Tips from Donald Trump

1. Never Stop Trying: "Never give up. Do not settle for remaining in your comfort zone. Remaining complacent is a good way to get nowhere."

2. Live in the Present: "I try to learn from the past, but I plan for the future by focusing exclusively on the present. That's where the fun is."

3. Think Grand Thoughts: "As long as you're going to be thinking anyway, think big."

4. Enjoy Your Work: "If you're interested in 'balancing' work and pleasure, stop trying to balance them. Instead, make your work more pleasurable."

5. Be Positive with Every Turn of Events: "What separates the winners from the losers is how a person reacts to each new twist of fate."[72]

Those are very good success tips, and you can see how Jose does something very similar. I will list them for you one by one.

5 Ways Jose Pursues Success

1. Never Stop Trying: Jose never gives up. Each time he has a difficult circumstance, he finds out what he needs to do and then does it. Never has he given up.

2. Live in the Present: Jose does the work that he needs to do for each day, and then he spends time with his family. He does not waste time wishing things were different. He does not grow discontented wishing for the future.

3. Think Grand Thoughts: Jose knows what his business should do next. First, he wanted to be legal. Then he wanted to hire employees. He knows when it is time to grow.

4. Enjoy Your Work: Machinery is like a puzzle to Jose. He started work mowing lawns, but he stayed with fixing equipment

because it interested him more. So he does something now that he enjoys.

5. Be Positive with Every Turn of Events: Jose can truly roll with the punches. When his worker was injured, Jose stayed with him at the hospital. He found out what he needed to do to compensate the employee and did that. Jose is always solving problems.

That is something important everyone should take from Jose. He knows that he will have problems in his business. And he knows who to call when those problems happen!

Jose will never give up because of a problem. One businessperson has some very good advice: "The more you embrace change and welcome challenges, the more you overcome fear. And, the more experiences you undergo, the less fear you have."[73] This kind of positive attitude is essential if you want to succeed as an immigrant to the Land of Business.

STAKING A CLAIM

EXPLANATIONS

Guiding a new startup business owner can get frustrating. As you know, you have to explain things so many times, but they come in as if you have never mentioned the things to them before. Jose did that to me so many times, but I kept on remembering something my dad told me.

My dad has learned nine different languages. People would say something like: "Wow, you have a good memory." But it was not a naturally good memory; it was hard work. My dad told me that he repeated his learning seven times before the knowledge would be really his.

So he always told me to be patient with others, because you have not yet repeated that information for the seventh time with the same person. I have never needed to repeat anything to any-one for seven times. Learning something new means that you are learning, not that you lack intelligence. I consider I deal with very smart folks like Jose.

THE SEMINAR

Jose emailed me this time: "One of my friends told me that I should be an S corp. I think I am C corp. Why I am a C corp?"

I emailed him back: "Jose, come to my office tonight. I am doing a seminar on C corp vs S corp. Bring your friend, too. A tax structure is like your outfit; what looks good on others might not look good on you. You have no paper and for some other reasons, too, you should be a C corp, not an S corp."

He showed up to my seminar and made notes. Later on, I saw him posting his notes on Facebook. He calls them his bible.

THE LEASE

Time goes so fast when life is busy and good. Jose texted me three years into operating as a C corp. He texted: "Jing, I found a place to move my shop to. The owner's name is Nick. Do you think I can get a lease from him? Should I tell him I have no paper?"

I texted to Jose: "Jose, the only time a landlord would need to know your immigration status is if they were asking you for a personal guarantee on the lease. When they see your tax return, your tax return will show the ID to be an ITIN, as they all start with the number 9. Other regular folks start with other kind of digits. Like in Iowa, a lot of folks have 4 to begin the social security number."

"Jing, what if he asks about my social security number? Should I just give to him the ITIN number? Do I need to come forward to tell him I do not have social security number? Would this hurt my ability to get the space?"

I sensed that I needed to text back a long and thorough explanation. "Normally not. As the landlord is looking at your company's fiscal history and you are doing so well, no one would have an issue with leasing a space to you.

"Just give him your EIN number, as DDH is the one leasing the space, not you personally. Landlord might ask for DDH's tax return. Since DDH is C corp, its tax return won't show your personal tax ID. Even if you go into partnership, normally the attorney will draft an agreement, and your partner should not need to know your personal ID.

"The ITIN is a tax ID. For anything related to taxes, this number will help to track your payment and tax liabilities. It is tied to your personal ID; so some folks without knowing the difference think it is a social security number. It starts with 9; so it is not a social security number."

I got back a thumbs up.

THE HOUSE

Jose and his wife came to see me. They were thinking of buying a home.

"Our son is already eight years old, and he needs more space," Mrs. Hernandez said.

Jose nodded. "We saved some money. The house we looked at, we have to borrow money to buy. What do we do? We have no papers."

You remember that when Jose and his wife came to the USA, this boy was a tiny baby that Mrs. Hernandez was holding. Jose had been living and working in the USA for eight years by this time. He had been paying taxes all that time, too. But the legal solutions for his business were not the same solutions for buying a house.

It is true that most banks would not do a mortgage loan with an ITIN holder. But some credit unions and small community state banks will consider it. Especially if you can give 50% of the house value as a down payment, then the bank is only risking the other 50%. Plus, the bank also has the first title of the house.

In this case, some banks would do a loan with an ITIN holder. So I asked the Hernandez family to go to a small community bank or credit union to try their luck. That would be the first choice.

I also explained to them that they could do a seller financing arrangement. The seller would provide the loan, and Jose would pay the down payment to the seller. The county record of the house would show both Jose's and the prior owner's name. Once Jose finished paying the house in full, the title would change to Jose 100%.

"When I pay property tax, would the government need my ITIN?" Jose asked.

He was just so sensitive to his status, and I felt the pain inside my heart. I wished that there was an immigration program to offer to good human beings like Jose and his family. I wanted him to be at peace and stop worrying.

"No, Jose, you will get a coupon, or you can pay online. Don't be so nervous about your ITIN. You literally can use that number for your ID. What the ITIN does not do for you is that it does not accumulate the Social Security benefits for you at the Social Security Administration."

Mr. and Mrs. Hernandez left their appointment with me feeling much better.

A couple of days later, Jose came back. "Jing- we got the house financed through IED Credit Union! They did not even ask too much down payment as they valuate the house more than the price we are buying for. So we only need to pay 10% of the price. Now can I deduct the mortgage interest as I have no paper?"

"Yes, you can," I nodded, "just like all Americans do."

EQUIPMENT

Jose was surprised with paying use tax. Jose bought a machine at an auction in Omaha. He said, "The guy was telling me to pay sales tax myself when I came to pick up the equipment. What does that mean?"

I explained to Jose that he might be subject to use tax if this equipment is to be used by himself, not for resale.

"Of course I buy it for myself!" he proclaimed.

"Okay, and that is the use tax I mentioned to you before. You file a use tax return for that. You already charge your client sales tax when you do repairs, but if you buy things for your store, you need to pay use tax. If you did not pay it at purchase, then you just pay it yourself afterwards, and it is called use tax filing. Don't forget to file it, or I can help you. Just bring me the bill that you paid so that I can make sure the use tax was not already collected by the seller."

JOSE THE TAXPAYER

The first-year corporation income tax filing was so refreshing to Jose, as he made fairly good money. DDH ended up having tax liability payments to both federal and state governments after paying employee wages and other expenses. DDH was making its contribution to the governments.

After the taxes were paid, Jose asked me, "Is it time to pay myself from the leftover?"

It was. Jose properly and proudly took $25,000 from the company bank account as a dividend payment to himself. The $25,000 was taxed on his 1040 form as dividend income.

On the DDH corporation return, he paid taxes happily, as he considered this the American way of doing business. He was thrilled that he could actually pay taxes. He kept on reminding me: "Jing, I want to do everything right."

THE LAND OF BUSINESS

Jose succeeded as an immigrant twice. First, he emigrated to America. He did it in a different way, but he has done all he can to operate legally here. Jose has had more of a conscience about operating legally here than some natural born Americans.

And after emigrating to America, Jose became an immigrant a second time- a business immigrant. This time was not from Mexico to America. This time was from the Country of the Hand to the Land of Business.

A BOOK FOR JOSE

Jose has been in every chapter in this book. Something has happened every step of the way to call his attention to one of the principles I have included here. I feel in some ways that I have written this book for Jose and people like him.

These new immigrants to the Land of Business need to consider each point carefully. Do they have a burning desire to start a business? What kind of business should they start? What kind of product or service should they sell?

What kind of tax structure fits the business? Do they need a loan? Should they take on a partner? When should they hire their first employee? What kinds of taxes should they expect to pay?

Each of these questions we have considered in this book. And we have found answers together to each of them. If you have completed the reflections in the book, then you know much more about yourself as a person and as a business owner. You will have fewer problems and make fewer costly mistakes.

A PRACTICE OF BUSINESS AND AWARENESS

Eckhart Tolle tells the story of a man who won a new car in a lottery. His friends and family were all excited for him. "Isn't that good?" they exclaimed.

"Maybe," he answered.[74]

The man drove the car for several weeks before a drunk driver crashed into him. The car was destroyed, and the man was badly hurt. His friends and family came to the hospital to visit him and talk about the accident. "Isn't that terrible?" they exclaimed.

"Maybe," he answered.

While the man was still in the hospital healing, a landslide crushed his house. Everything he owned was destroyed. But because he was in the hospital, he did not die in the tragedy. Amazed by the coincidence, "Isn't that wonderful?" his friends and family exclaimed.

"Maybe," he answered.

The man could remain calm and unmoved by circumstances that we would call good or bad because he realized that no one knows the future. Life is always changing. If we can change with it and remain grateful and aware in every change, we will benefit from it. We will always be able to be at peace.

Richard Romanoff, CEO and President of Nebraskaland, looks at things this way. "Problems are a good thing. Any company that doesn't have its share of complicated problems probably doesn't have a very hearty business...But in the middle of difficulty lies opportunity. When things are going good, no one wants change. Greet difficulty as an opportunity for creative and financial enhancement."[75]

Whether things in the Land of Business look wonderful or devastating, you can make the best of them if you remain grateful and aware. Know that you are in the midst of great abundance and great opportunity. And whatever happens in the Land of Business, remember that you will be able to handle it if you just remember your *Appointment with Ying @ 8am.*

REFLECTION #17: YOUR BUSINESS STORY

The story of Jose's business is very instructive. Looking at your own story can be instructive, too.

	YOUR BUSINESS STORY
1	Write the story of your business, no matter what stage of it is happening now. Start with the things about you in your childhood and after that drew you to this business. Go through the dreaming and starting stages to wherever you are now.
2	Write the story of your business as a fable. Pretend that you are an immigrant from the Country of the Head, the Heart, or the Hand coming to the Land of Business. Make the events that happen to you take the shape of this kind of fantasy. What do you learn about yourself from putting your story into the form of a fable?

REFLECTION #18: OUR BUSINESS MENTORS

Throughout this book, we have focused on three of my role models: Elon Musk, Eckhart Tolle, and Donald Trump. They are very different men. Yet they have all taught me valuable lessons about business.

	YOUR BUSINESS MENTORS
1	What have you learned about strategy in business from Donald Trump? What lessons from the Country of the Head has he showed you?
2	What have you learned about creativity in business from Elon Musk? What lessons from the Country of the Hand has he showed you?
3	What have you learned about awareness in business from Eckhart Tolle? What lessons from the Country of the Heart has he showed you?
4	Which role models from the business world do you think you are most identified with? What lessons have you learned from them?

5	*Which clients of mine do you feel are most like you? What help have you gotten from watching them learn about the Land of Business?*

APPENDIX 1
CHAPTER 1 TEST ANSWERS

Add up the numbers (1 point for each type of passport) of HEART, HAND, and HEAD answers that you chose. The largest number is the Passport you hold. If you tied, redo the selection again the next day, and keep in mind that your choice should be your first thought; do not overthink.

CHAPTER 1 TEST ANSWERS			
1	*Hand*	*Head*	*Heart*
2	*Hand*	*Heart*	*Head*
3	*Head*	*Hand*	*Heart*
4	*Heart*	*Head*	*Hand*
5	*Heart*	*Head*	*Hand*
6	*Head*	*Hand*	*Heart*
7	*Heart*	*Hand*	*Head*
8	*Hand*	*Head*	*Heart*
9	*Hand*	*Head*	*Heart*
10	*Hand*	*Head*	*Heart*
11	*Heart*	*Head*	*Head*
12	*Head*	*Heart*	*Hand*
13	*Heart*	*Hand*	*Head*
14	*Heart*	*Hand*	*Head*
15	*Heart*	*Head*	*Hand*
16	*Heart*	*Head*	*Hand*
17	*Hand*	*Head*	*Heart*

Appendix 2
Select Character Index

The characters listed below were used to illustrate the different business orientations of business immigrants. However, not all characters mentioned in this book were identified to be one of the three.

Land of the Heart

Eckhart Tolle
Ying Sa
Stacie
Peter and Meg Keobunta
Luck Nguyen
Fei (Hua Hua's sister in law)
Nonprofit Owner in Bank Bully
Will

Land of the Head

Donald Trump
Hua Hua
Emily
Tony (The Cheese Gamble)
Leo (Partner with Francis)
Credit Card Shuffle Brothers
Charles
Ski Bump Couple
Lana (small banking)

LAND OF THE HAND

Elon Musk
Jose Hernandez
Denise
Tom
John (Hua Hua's brother)
Francis (Partner with Leo)
Samuel
Phillip
Nail Shop Owner
Auto Mechanic (15-year mistake)

Bibliography

McKenzie, Hamish. *Insane Mode: How Elon Musk's Tesla Sparked an Electric Revolution to End the Age of Oil.* New York: Dutton, 2018.

Tolle, Eckhart. *A New Earth: Awakening to Your Life's Purpose.* New York: Plume, 2005.

Tolle, Eckhart. *The Power of Now: A Guide to Spiritual Enlightenment.* Novato, CA: New World Library, 1999.

Trump, Donald. *The Way to the Top: The Best Business Advice I Ever Received.* New York: Crown Business, 2004.

Trump, Donald and Tony Schwartz. *The Art of the Deal.* New York: Random House, 1987.

Vance, Ashlee. *Elon Musk: Tesla, SpaceX, and the Quest for a Fantastic Future.* New York: HarperCollins, 2015.

ENDNOTES

1. https://en.wikipedia.org/wiki/Eckhart_Tolle
2. https://www.youtube.com/watch?v=wH6FdFiUueU&list=-PLEguIFSuqm6iNL9Eir4ygPdrkSMQlsPOW&index=5&t=0s
3. https://www.britannica.com/biography/Elon-Musk
4. Vance, Elon Musk, 54-55.
5. Trump, Art, 33.
6. Trump, Art, 3.
7. Vance, Elon Musk, 72.
8. Vance, Elon Musk, 75-78.
9. Vance, Elon Musk, 84-85.
10. Vance, Elon Musk, 24.
11. https://en.wikipedia.org/wiki/Eckhart_Tolle
12. Trump, Art, 59-63.
13. From Josie Natori, Founder and CEO of Natori Company, in Trump, The Way to the Top, 178.
14. https://www.investopedia.com/updates/donald-trump-success-story/
15. Trump, Art, 73.
16. Trump, The Way to the Top, 253.
17. https://www.youtube.com/watch?v=9Tih_SrzXA0&list=-PLEguIFSuqm6iNL9Eir4ygPdrkSMQlsPOW&index=6&t=0s
18. Joseph T. Charles, President of Charles Industries, Ltd. In Trump, The Way to the Top, 52.
19. Vance, Elon Musk, 98-112.
20. Vance, Elon Musk, 150-155.
21. https://en.wikipedia.org/wiki/S_corporation
22. Vance, Elon Musk, 206.
23. Vance, Elon Musk, 204-211.

24. Harris E. DeLoach, Jr., President and CEO of Sonoco in Trump, The Way to the Top, 80.

25. Trump, The Way to the Top, 29.

26. Trump, Art, 86.

27. Trump, Art, 95.

28. Vance, Elon Musk, 71-72.

29. Vance, Elon Musk, 82-88.

30. Vance, Elon Musk, 105-107.

31. Vance, Elon Musk, 167-172.

32. https://cleantechnica.com/2017/06/23/tesla-co-founder-marc-tarpenning-tells-definitive-story-companys-beginnings/

33. Tolle, A New Earth, 65-84.

34. Tolle, A New Earth, 112.

35. Thomas M. Joyce, President and CEO of Knight Trading Company in Trump, The Way to the Top, 135.

36. Trump, The Way to the Top, 88.

37. Trump, The Way to the Top, 25.

38. Vance, Elon Musk, 61-62.

39. Trump, The Way to the Top, 165.

40. Trump, Art, 21.

41. Trump, The Way to the Top, 34.

42. Tolle, A New Earth, 38-41.

43. Richard "Bo" Dietl, Chairman of Beau Dietl & Associates says, in Trump, The Way to the Top, 83.

44. Trump, Art, 59.

45. Trump, Art, 146.

46. Trump, Art, 146-147.

47. Donald L. Drakeman, President and CEO of Medarex, Inc. in Trump, The Way to the Top, 85.

48. Trump, Art, 243.

49. Tolle, A New Earth, 223-224.

50. Gerald D. Edwards, President and CEO of Engineered Plastic Products, Inc. in Trump, The Way to the Top, 91-92.

51. Tolle, A New Earth, 139.

52. Vance, Elon Musk, 16-17.

53. Vance, Elon Musk, 218.

54. Vance, Elon Musk, 21.

55. Vance, Elon Musk, 222.

56. Vance, Elon Musk, 220-221.

57. Vance, Elon Musk, 130.

58. Mayo A. Shattuck III, Chairman, President, and CEO of Constellation Energy Group in Trump, The Way to the Top, 217.

59. Trump, The Way to the Top, 111.

60. Trump, The Way to the Top, 248.

61. https://en.wikipedia.org/wiki/Riverside_South,_Manhattan

62. Vance, Elon Musk, 75-77.

63. Vance, Elon Musk, 80-81.

64. Vance, Elon Musk, 84.

65. https://home.barclays/who-we-are/our-history/

66. https://www.sapling.com/2076636/obtain-banking-license

67. Trump, The Way to the Top, 220.

68. Tolle, A New Earth, 236-238.

69. https://www.pbs.org/thinktank/transcript1292.html

70. Vance, Elon Musk, 25-28.

71. Vance, Elon Musk, 43-44, 51.

72. http://www.smbceo.com/2016/01/15/5-success-tips-from-donald-trump/

73. Steven Plochocki, CEO of InSight Health Corporation in Trump, The Way to the Top, 200.

74. Tolle, A New Earth, 197.

75. Trump, The Way to the Top, 207.

Acknowledgments

There is another hero of mine, and I want you to meet him properly. He is my husband Steve. On May 23, 2003, an unexpected city construction accident happened in my neighborhood which sent 4 feet deep city sewage and storm water into our home within 3 hours' time while Steve and I were out of town with our little daughters.

Nothing was rescued, and everything in our study was gone.

Worst of all, the acid water submerged the entire computer system Steve has at home, which contained the only copies of multiple ready-to-publish research papers in the applied mathematics field. Steve was the rising star in his field, and he was recruited to be a tenured professor at Iowa State University. That was the sole reason our family left Toronto, Canada and relocated in Iowa.

All was gone with the flood. There was not much conversation between us, just a lot of pain. That was the first time I ever saw his tears.

At our wedding, one of his colleagues commented on Steve's career, and he said: "I would not be surprised that Steve gets a big prize for his research." I had high hopes to be a wife of a big prize winner, and losing these research papers meant a major blow to if not the end of his academic career. That hurt me and scared me deeply.

From that day on, secretively I worked to impress him of what I could do for him and for our family. So I started working as hard as I could in my field.

But Steve has been my invisible hands that handled every critical turn of Community CPA for the past 25 years. He was literally the reason why we are here today and why the book is here. He is my rock.

Community CPA is truly remarkable. Collectively we speak 9 different languages and originate from 10 different countries. For my readers, no wonder you will catch me speaking Chinglish or Spanglish and so on. Simply, Community CPA is a melting pot for language barriers. The culture diversity was naturally effortlessly melted into our business principles and practice. Without my staff, their quality services, and their commitment to our dear clients, this book would not be born.

The volunteers and board members of Immigrant Entrepreneurs Summit are important contributors to this book. They created this time and space for immigrant business owners to come together annually so they can see and walk a clear path to the American Dream. I witnessed the transformations this nonprofit organization brought to immigrant business communities. With admiration, I write this into my books.

And my children, thank you for your understanding of mom. Forgive me for never being around the dinner table when it was time to have dinner. May I use this book to explain how mom spent her time. I say sorry to all three of you and also promise you that I will make that up when I have my grandchildren.

To my friends and my clients, without you, there would not be a firm called Community CPA. You worked your magic through my hands and built this name for our community. Together we saved many dreams for business owners through our professional knowledge and abundant compassion.

I hope you have enjoyed the read! Please look up Commmunitycpa.com.

We are there for one reason- you!

YING SA | OCTOBER 2019

About Ying Sa

Ying Sa is the founder and Principal Certified Public Accountant at Community CPA. The firm provides tax, audit, accounting, business consultations and IT solutions to businesses and individuals across the United States, Canada, and around the world.

Ying was born in Beijing, China before becoming a citizen of Canada and then the United States of America. She got an accounting degree in Canada and worked as an accountant in Canada for several years before relocating to Iowa. Ying served six years as the Chief Financial Officer for the Iowa Manufacturing Extension Partnership at Iowa State University and five years as Vice President of Controllers for Wells Fargo Financial, Inc. in Des Moines, Iowa. She started Community CPA in 1998 and has been leading Community CPA full time since 2008.

Ying was featured in Accounting Today in 2019 for her contribution to the profession as well as to the community. The article named Ying "the Pillar of the Community." Ying was also featured in Thomson Reuters Solutions Magazine in 2017 for leading such a successful and dynamic CPA firm with global interest speaking 9 different languages and serving over 7,000 clients worldwide.

She has also been featured in the Des Moines Register and the Des Moines Business Record on numerous occasions as recognition for her tireless and selfless work on behalf of the community, as well as the success of Community CPA. In fact, on November 18, 2017, Ying was specifically honored for her commitment and dedication to the immigrant business communities in Iowa and the surrounding Midwest at the Immigrant Entrepreneurs Summit, a 501(c)3 nonprofit she co-founded and has chaired for the past decade.

In 2016, the Iowa Small Business Administration (SBA) presented Ying and Community CPA the 2016 Iowa Minority Small Business Champion of the Year award. In 2015, Ying received the 2015 Small Business of the Year award at the Greater Quad-Cities Hispanic Chamber of Commerce's Annual Gala. In May of 2013, the Governor appointed Ying to serve on the Board of Iowa Accountancy. Ying served on the board for five years.

Ying has been honored with many awards for her volunteerism, entrepreneurial, and community spirit. The following are just a few: Thomson Reuters' 2019 Loca Pacioli Accounting Award, SBA 2016 Iowa Minority Small Business Champion of the Year Award, Greater Quad-Cities Hispanic Chamber of Commerce's 2015 Small Business of Year Award, the Iowa Business Record's "2010 Woman of Influence," Iowa 2010 Volunteer Hall of Fame, and the 2008 Jim Goodman Entrepreneurial Spirit Award from East Des Moines Chamber of Commerce.

Ying has successfully helped numerous large corporations, nonprofits, small businesses and individuals with a broad range of complicated tax and accounting issues. She enjoys interacting with people of all backgrounds and cultures, and she is passionate and generous about sharing her expertise with her clients. As a successful immigrant woman with broad corporate and business experience, Ying masterfully blends her unique life experiences and perspectives into her own professional work and her service to clients.

Upon meeting Ying, her devotion and passion to the industry and the community become immediately apparent. Her expertise, experience, compassion, and professionalism provide an unparalleled level of service that builds long lasting trust and relationships.

Ying lives in Des Moines with her family. Her husband Steve is a retired full professor of applied mathematics and currently a partner of Community CPA. Her daughter Stephanie is currently a law school student at Stanford Law School. Her daughter Crystal graduated from Carnegie Mellon with a bachelor's degree in Statistics and now is a student at Sheridan College in Oakville, Ontario, Canada majoring in animation. Her son Andy is a student at the University of Iowa majoring in Creative Writing and Computer Science.

Appointment with Ying @ 8am: Starting Up a Business is Ying's first book. Others planned in the series include *Appointment with Ying @ 10am: Developing a Business; Appointment with Ying @ 2pm: Expanding a Business;* and *Appointment with Ying @ 6pm: Retiring from Business.*

COMMUNITY
CPA●COM

DES MOINES OFFICE
3816 Ingersoll Avenue, Des Moines, IA 50312
Phone: (515) 288-3188 | Fax: (515) 271-8889
Email: cpa@communitycpa.com
Office hours: 8:30am- 5:30pm Mon.- Sat.

CORALVILLE OFFICE
2421 Coral Court, Suite 1, Coralville, IA 52241
Phone: (319) 208-3712 | Fax: (515) 271-8889
Email: cpa@communitycpa.com
Office hours: 8:30am- 5:30pm Mon.- Fri.

BLOOMINGTON OFFICE
3001 Metro Dr. Suite 260, Bloomington MN 55425
Phone: (612) 808-9418 | Fax: (888) 964-8770
Email: cpa@communitycpa.com
Office hours: 8:30am- 5:30pm Mon.- Fri.

Contact us today!

CPSIA information can be obtained
at www.ICGtesting.com
Printed in the USA
FSHW010129211119
64326FS

9 781647 133290